Collected

SARA COLERIDGE, the daughter of Sa[...] at Keswick, in the Lake District, [...] published work (1822) was a transla[...] in collaboration with her brother De[...] ment, she married her first cousin Henry Nelson Coleridge (1798-1843) in September 1829. The Coleridges lived in London, where Henry practised law. Sara's first child Herbert was born in 1830, and her second, Edith, in 1832. Her mental and physical health had been fragile since childhood, and the death of her newborn twins in 1834 increased her depression and reliance on opium. In 1834 she published a popular collection of verse for children, and in 1837 the fairytale romance *Phantasmion*. After the death of Samuel Taylor Coleridge in 1834 Sara and her husband embarked on the huge task of editing and publishing his works, a project that Sara continued in collaboration with Derwent after Henry Nelson Coleridge's death in 1842. She also continued to write her own works, leaving a large collection of unpublished poems, essays and journals at her death in 1852.

PETER SWAAB studied at the universities of Cambridge, Harvard and New York, and currently teaches at University College London. He has published on literature of the Romantic and Victorian periods, including *Lives of the Great Romantics: Wordsworth* (Pickering and Chatto, 1996), and an edition of Edward Lear's nonsense and travel writings, *Over the Land and Over the Sea* (Carcanet, 2005).

FyfieldBooks aim to make available some of the great classics of British and European literature in clear, affordable formats, and to restore often neglected writers to their place in literary tradition.

FyfieldBooks take their name from the Fyfield elm in Matthew Arnold's 'Scholar Gypsy' and 'Thyrsis'. The tree stood not far from the village where the series was originally devised in 1971.

> *Roam on! The light we sought is shining still.*
> *Dost thou ask proof? Our tree yet crowns the hill,*
> *Our Scholar travels yet the loved hill-side*

from 'Thyrsis'

SARA COLERIDGE

Collected Poems

Edited with an introduction by
PETER SWAAB

Fyfield*Books*

CARCANET

Acknowledgements

The research for this book was supported by a Research Leave award from the Arts and Humanities Research Council (AHRC). I am also grateful to the Harry Ransom Humanities Research Center for the award of a Mellon Fellowship, and to the English Department at UCL for sabbatical leave.

For permission, and indeed encouragement, to publish these poems, my thanks to the late Joan Coleridge and her daughter, Mrs Priscilla Cassam.

I am grateful to many friends and academic colleagues for various kinds of help: Rosemary Ashton, James Ball, Martha Campbell, Jonathan Crewe, Dennis Low, Pat Fox, Alison Girling, Judith Hawley, Philip Horne, Danny Karlin, Alison Light, Andrew McDonald, Charlotte Mitchell, Claire Preston, Peter Robinson, Nicholas Roe, Richard Swaab, Henry Woudhuysen, and Melissa Zeiger. Kevin Jackson was especially important in seeing that the project got going, and Judith Willson, my editor at Carcanet, in seeing that it got finished.

First published in Great Britain in 2007 by
Carcanet Press Limited
Alliance House
Cross Street
Manchester M2 7AQ

A CIP catalogue record for this book is available from the British Library
ISBN 978 1 85754 895 2

The publisher acknowledges financial assistance from Arts Council England

Typeset by XL Publishing Services, Tiverton
Printed and bound in England by SRP Ltd, Exeter

Contents

Collected Poems of Sara Coleridge

(★ indicates previously published works)

Poems 1829–1843

Introduction

It would be delightful if her centenary [...] might result in an edition of her poems, of which I understand some were never published; and I know that others in her *Phantasmion* are uncommonly good.

(Edmund Blunden)[1]

Among the Sara Coleridge papers in the Harry Ransom Center in Texas are these verses in the hand of Sara's daughter Edith dated 29 March 1852. Five weeks later, Sara was dead.

Doggrel Charm

To a little lump of malignity, on being medically assured that it was not a fresh growth, but an old growth splitting.

1

Split away, split away, split away, split!
Plague of my life, delay pretermit!
Rapidly, rapidly, rapidly go!
Haste ye to mitigate trouble and woe!

2

Then if you come again, done be His will
Who ordereth all things beyond human skill!
Patience he findeth who seeketh that need
Grace from the fountainhead comes at full speed.

3

Crack away, tumour, I pray thee to crack,
Just now you seem to be on the right track
But if you're in the wrong, right let me be,
And promptly submitting to Heaven's decree.

This is a poem near the end of its tether, but it has art in its arrangement, as each stanza moves from a ragged and even doggerelly metric to a final line which would not be out of place in a nineteenth-century hymn. The last stanza, in particular, almost loses its metrical way until

---

1 'The Daughter of Coleridge', manuscript dated 5 March 1952, housed in the Harry Ransom Humanities Research Center (henceforth, HRC).

it arrives at its resigned conclusion. It is a nervous poem, havering between jollity and hysteria; and a poem about courage and piety, exemplifying both. 'On the right track', for instance, voices a wan hope for recovery but is also a steady euphemism for death. Recovery and death are both in their different ways 'the right track' for a Christian imagining the life to come. 'I pray thee' is a parody of a social courtesy, an apt form of address since a tumour is at once foreign to you and yet part of yourself, an invader with whom you can be – you can't *not* be – on ghastly familiar terms.[2] But is also a genuine prayer, knowing that a tumour which bears illness may also be an agent of the religious truth of afflictions undergone.

Sara has headed these lines 'Doggrel Charm', but it is not exactly a charm: it knows well enough that the powers of verse lack the magic to cure mortal disease. And if it is hardly what we would usually call an accomplished poem, it isn't doggerel either. It's a poem I've not been able to forget since I came across it seven years ago in Texas, and it was one of the things that made me want to search out her other writings, and in the end to edit her poetry. For all that the occasion of these lines is poignantly extreme, and that Sara herself classified them as doggerel, they are in some ways characteristic of her poetry: for instance in their contest between self-pity and stoicism, in their religious seriousness and emotional openness, and in their sense of metrical possibilities.

Despite the admiration of Blunden and a handful of others, Sara Coleridge's poetry has had to wait more than 150 years to be published as a collection, and she is meagerly represented, when at all, in several recent anthologies of nineteenth-century women's poetry, including some which have gone well off the beaten track to publish writers forgotten since their own day.[3] But she is a considerable poet, passionate, versatile, and brainy: 'uncommonly good', indeed. She makes a notable link between the Romantic and Victorian periods, and not just thanks to her name. She is Romantic enough to be drawn repeatedly to imagining the paradisal ('bright', 'gleam' and 'heav'n' are favourite words), and Romantic also in working to see how the mind can build a heaven in hell's despite;

2   There are comparable tones of grim humour and dark intimacy in Harold Pinter's poem 'Cancer Cells', first published in the *Guardian* on 14 March 2002 (reprinted in *Various Voices: Prose, Poetry, Politics 1948–2005* (2005), p. 172).

3   She does not feature, for instance, in two useful collections, *Romantic Women Poets 1788–1848*, edited by Andrew Ashfield (1998), and *Romantic Women Poets: An Anthology*, edited by Duncan Wu (1997); and the Oxford *Nineteenth-Century Women's Poetry*, edited by Isobel Armstrong and Joseph Bristow (1996), includes only three poems, one more than Quiller-Couch put in his *Oxford Book of English Verse* back in 1919.

Victorian in her readiness to translate disappointment into stoically acknowledged Christian truths, and in her distrust of morbid self-preoccupation. Her main themes are grand enough: the seasons of life; innocence and experience; the meaning of affliction; the links between the earthly and the heavenly; the truth of dreams and dreaming. The best poems have both weight and intensity.[4]

Texts and Sources

This volume collects all Sara Coleridge's completed poems for non-juvenile readers which I have been able to find, together with transcriptions of her more substantial drafts and fragments. She herself made the task easier by copying a substantial amount of the completed work into a red leather-bound album, now housed in the Harry Ransom Center in Austin, Texas, together with the larger part of her literary remains. This album, which she sometimes called the 'Red Book', includes transcriptions of 87 poems. It also lists the titles (but not the text) of the 35 poems included in *Phantasmion*, the extraordinary children's story which she published in 1837. These make up together the greater part of the 185 poems included here, of which 120 are now published for the first time.[5] Aside from *Phantasmion* and the Red Book, the main source of Sara's poetry is the series of five volumes of children's verses which she copied out in 1834. A selection from these was published as *Pretty Lessons in Verse for Good Children* (1834). The five books of children's verses mainly comprise a selection of the 399 'Herby cards' on which Sara wrote short verses for her son Herbert,[6] little pieces written on calling cards, invitations, and the like, mostly verses of between four and sixteen lines, depending on the size of the cards. Together, the five volumes include more than 160 verses, of which a few were adapted for *Phantasmion* or copied into the Red Book, and 34 found their way into *Pretty Lessons* (which contained 53 verses in all). *Pretty Lessons* was a commercial success, and in 1848 Sara was planning a further selec-

---

4 For the reader who would like to go straight to some of these best, I suggest 'Verses written in sickness 1833...', 'Poppies', 'The Water Lily', 'Grief's heavy hand hath swayed the lute' (*Phantasmion*), 'O sleep, my babe, hear not the rippling wave' (*Phantasmion*), 'The winds were whispering, the waters glistering' (*Phantasmion*), 'For my Father on his lines called "Work Without Hope"', 'Dreams. II. Time's Acquittal', 'Dreams. III.To a Friend', 'To my Son', and 'The melancholy Prince'.

5 Poems previously published are marked with an asterisk on the contents page, and the endnotes in all cases give details of first publication.

6 For further bibliographical details, see pp. 17–18 and 212.

tion of her children's verse as a follow-up volume, but the plans came to nothing.[7] Most of the verses are designed for her own children, aids to learning grammar, animal's names, Latin vocabulary, geography, and so on, as well as some fables and stories. Sara believed that good children's verse could stand adult scrutiny, and the boundary between children's poetry and adult poetry is not an absolute one; but even so, I have included only a selection of the children's verse in this edition, on grounds of space, and on the grounds that they are recognisably different in kind from her other poems. Some of the poems in the children's volumes, however, express adult feelings of dejection, foreboding, and complaint (and might well be thought too dark for small children): I have included all of these.

The most important section of the Red Book is headed 'Poems of Sara Coleridge in Widowhood', and is prefaced with a short note:

My conversations with Mr de Vere in the years 1843,4,5, our discussions of Wordsworth especially, re-excited my little weak poetic faculty. The poemets which were produced under this influence, I shall mark thus – *for A. de V.* – as they were sent to him in letters during our early correspondence. Some verses I wrote in books which I gave him – some on my feelings about death after the loss of Henry I have no copy of.

Not poems, then, but 'poemets', and even the presumption of this is mitigated by the sponsoring presences of de Vere and Wordsworth. Sara's modesty seems excessive, even for somebody with a high Coleridgean sense of what really constituted 'a poem' worthy of the name. It is one side of a literary career which combined unusual self-assertion with sometimes fierce self-deprecation. She was later to look back on her own poetry once again in an affecting letter she wrote to Derwent on 7 November 1851, during her last illness, which he marked 'very precious' and 'to be carefully preserved': 'I began a wild poem once.[8] I sometimes wish I had not been diverted from it, and spent so much time on theology, which I was partly led on to by my friend, de Vere.' Here she inserts a dagger signalling a marginal note: 'There are a few poems worth little but characteristic as a set in a red leather M.S. book', and then a further note opposite the date and address elaborates: 'The poems in the red book are worth little – but

7   In a letter of February or March 1848 Sara wrote to her sister-in-law Mary about this second collection: '…can you speak, as I mentioned, to Mr Evans about *them there* juvenile poemets? You understand, tho' one cannot quite state that plainly for fear of hurting one's bargain, that my sole *hopjack* is the little sum of money I may gain by the booklet' (HRC).
8   I take this to be 'Howithorn'. See headnote on pp. 199–201.

have a *character* – taken together with the Phantasmion songs.' Then finally, cross-written on the first page, 'merely *curious* as the production of Poet Coleridge's daughter – curious psychologically'.[9] There are evidently powerfully mixed feelings here, with pointers to Derwent about how best to present the poems, along with pointers that actually they are not worth presenting. The letter starts with remarks about the frequency of disappointment in literary careers, the context being Derwent's two-volume gathering their late brother Hartley Coleridge's poetry. But if this was a hint to Derwent to carry on with the sibling editorial work, it was not one he acted on.

Although Sara was not a prolific poet, she was a fluent one. She wrote poems during all her life, but there were three particularly productive periods. The first of these was her long (and long-distance) engagement to her cousin Henry, during which she sent many verses in or as letters; the second was the early childhood of Herbert and Edith; and the third period, prompted by her friendship with the young Irish poet (and fervent Wordsworthian) Aubrey de Vere, followed the death of her husband in 1843. She might be thought an occasional poet, in the sense that she had a ready poetic faculty which seized on the occasions that presented themselves.

When Derwent Coleridge edited the poetry of his late brother Hartley, he devoted the first of his two volumes to Hartley's 1833 collection, and arranged the contents of Volume 2 under a variety of headings: 'Miscellaneous Sonnets', 'Sonnets of the Seasons', 'Sonnets and other poems on birds, insects and flowers', 'Sonnets and other poems referring to the period of Infancy and Childhood', 'Meditative and Descriptive poems. – Memorial Pieces', 'Miscellaneous Poems, Chiefly Lyrical', 'Playful and Humorous Pieces', 'Translations', 'Prometheus. A Fragment', 'Sketches of English Poets', and 'Scriptural and Religious Subjects'. Derwent was partly following the elaborate classes into which Wordsworth arranged his own poems in his later collections, a practice which Sara deprecated, as we shall see. But the categories are worth noting, because taken together they well suggest the range of Sara's own poems. Although she was not a sonneteer, the reader of this volume will find much about the seasons, childhood, infancy, animals; a number of memorial pieces; and also humorous poems, translations, sketches of poets, and poems on religious subjects. Like Hartley, then, she was a minor poet but one with considerable range.

---

9   Compare her letter of 27 April 1834 to Emily Trevenen: 'Crabbe's life by his son is very interesting, and it is quite the work of the *son* of a genius: something fresh and peculiar in the *air* of the thing, though without the power and brilliancy of the father's mind' (HRC). Coleridge himself had called 'Kubla Khan' 'a psychological curiosity'.

The Three Periods of Sara Coleridge's Poetry

I have grouped Sara Coleridge's poems into three sections, corresponding to the major epochs of her life. First, 'Early Poems 1815–1829', taking her from age thirteen as far as her marriage in September 1829. Secondly, 'Poems 1829–1843', the period of her marriage and of the prolific outpouring of her verses for her children. Thirdly, 'Poems 1843–1852', from her widowhood in January 1843 until her own death.

Almost all of the 'Early Poems' are taken from the Red Book, in which they had been lovingly transcribed by Henry Nelson Coleridge during the period of his and Sara's long betrothal. They met in December 1822, and were secretly engaged within three months. Henry's family did not countenance the match, but the couple were resolute, despite being so far separated (Sara lived in the Lake District, Henry in London). Eventually Henry's father James Duke Coleridge gave his consent, and the pair were married in September 1829.[10]

Sara's early poems are graceful and elegant, but are in many ways the typical album verses of an accomplished young woman. As a sort of one-sided record in verse of their long affair, they suggest its narrative rather in the manner of an epistolary novel. They give an interesting record of a respectable but enormously prolonged late Georgian courtship, complete with its moments of uncertainty and fluctuations of intimacy and trust. Many of the verses were sent in letters:

> O, how, Love, must I fill
> This dreary, dreary blank –
> How do your eyes no ill,
> Yet fully use my frank?

She manages a witty turn on their epistolary plight in 'Th'enamoured Nymph, whose faithful voice':

> Each kiss he sends with kindness winning
>   She echoes by a kiss as fond; –
> Nature prevents her from beginning,
>   But lets her sweetly correspond.[11]

Among the later poems in this section the best are perhaps 'Epistle

---

10 See Earl Leslie Griggs, *Coleridge Fille* (1940), pp. 42–66, for a much fuller narrative.
11 See pp. 49 and 53 respectively.

from Sara to her sister Mary' and 'The Rose of Love my Henry sends'.

If Henry was the addressee of these early poems, that place was taken during the years of her marriage by her children, and in Sara's later works by Aubrey de Vere. I will discuss the children's poems in the next section, and say a brief word here about the later writings and their frequent inspirer. An ardent and romantic figure, the Irish poet de Vere was twelve years Sara's junior, and the poems written during their closest intimacy nearly all start from her romantically grieved feelings about her seniority, and her classical acknowledgment of the seasons of life. Little of their correspondence survives (de Vere objected to private letters becoming public), and what there is we have only in the passages which Edith Coleridge selected for the *Memoir and Letters* of her mother, for which she tended to divest the letters of anything offensive or indiscreet. De Vere's *Recollections* (1897), moreover, are not revealing. But Sara's emotionally candid poems make it clear that she was moved to think once again about the possibility of a new love in her life, even if she mainly dismissed the idea even in the moment of entertaining it. The poems marked 'For A. de V' are her most eloquent expressions of yearning and of resignation, and her most tempered explorations of the meeting between the ideal and the real.

Juvenile Readers

The question of 'juvenile' and 'non-juvenile' readers begs the question, for somebody who admired and followed the *Lyrical Ballads* as closely as Sara Coleridge, of what *is* a poem for a juvenile reader. Songs *of* innocence may well not be songs *by* innocence, and they may not be meant exclusively for innocents. 'Poppies', for instance:

> The Poppies blooming all around
> My Herbert loves to see;
> Some pearly white, some dark as night,
> Some red as cramasie:
>
> He loves their colours fresh and fine,
> As fair as fair may be;
> But little does my darling know
> How good they are to me.
>
> He views their clust'ring petals gay,
> And shakes their nut-brown seeds;
> But they to him are nothing more
> Than other brilliant weeds.

O! how shouldst thou, with beaming brow,
　With eye and cheek so bright,
Know aught of that gay blossom's power,
　Or sorrows of the night?

When poor Mama long restless lies,
　She drinks the poppy's juice;
That liquor soon can close her eyes,
　And slumber soft produce:

O then my sweet, my happy boy
　Will thank the Poppy-flower,
Which brings the sleep to dear Mama,
　At midnight's darksome hour.

The gap between the child's innocence and the mother's experience moves the poem in various emotional directions: to a dark intimation of the adult body and its needs and greeds, evoked in that lusciously stored-up poeticism 'cramasie' (crimson); to secretiveness, since a part of decent parenting is not telling your children everything; to a confessional eagerness which is one consequence of such secretiveness; and to something like envy of the child's blitheness. The poem celebrates the child's innocence, but it also does the rather darker work of imaginatively taking it away. As the third person of 'My Herbert' and 'he' becomes the second person of 'thou' (line 13), so Herbert is brought closer to his mother's unhappiness. We cannot tell if the fifth verse is spoken by Herbert or Sara, if the phrase 'poor Mama' voices his sympathy or her self-sympathy. But the last stanza imagines Herbert's state of future knowledge, one which – thanks to the poppies – will keep him 'happy', and also handily justify her drug habit. There is something macabre but not uninteresting in this, as in much of the best poetry about adult and child encounters. It suggests, for instance, the frequent emotional loneliness of adults spending their time with immature persons, and it has an undercurrent of what it well knows to be unfair exasperation. It is an unexpected work to appear in a book called *Pretty Lessons in Verse for Good Children* (the mawkish title came from Henry, whose initiative and insistence it was to get it published). Herbert is its imagined but not exactly its real addressee, except that as one of the 'good children' he may have read the book.[12]

12 He would have been well able to, even at age four. He was a brilliant schoolboy and a remarkable scholar, acting as secretary of the committee which inaugurated the New English Dictionary, before his premature death at 31. He gave much of the credit for his academic success to his mother's educational methods.

'Poppies' was not the only melancholy poem among the children's verses. The second volume opens with an intensely dejected series of eight poems seemingly written under the apprehension that she would die.[13] In some of these Sara seems to be imagining her children reading the poems after her own death, and they are meant as messages of farewell and religious consolation for her children once they would reach an age to take them in. She explains her illness, her love for her children and her regret at leaving them. One motivation behind these poignant verses may have been to articulate her distress to her own children as her father had *not* done for her. In starting a new manuscript volume with these dark verses, Sara makes it into something akin to a book of her own poetry, before it more reassuringly becomes a sequel to the first volume of children's poems. But is is notable that she did not transcribe these poems of dejection and illness into the Red Book, reluctant perhaps to record such extreme times in her emotional history.[14]

Many of the poems present emotional landscapes quite opposite to this, radiant scenes of parentless play in nature, with a sometimes Blakean sense of the sensuous and abundant surrounding world. There are stories of venturing, of narrow escapes, of pride coming before a fall, though often she is reluctant to make the moral blatant, and one poem ends with the reflection that lessons are better learnt 'without a wordy commentary'.[15] A few verses arrive, with pre-Darwinian candour, at quite gruesome outcomes, sometimes but not always narrated with comic gusto. In the more extreme instances she gives us cragfast sheep likely to die, and lambs waiting for the ravens to come and peck their eyes out. A series of botanical poems on the naming of flowers are probably influenced by Wordsworth's sequence 'On the Naming of Places'. In general these children's poems have qualities which the album verses of the 1820s lacked. They are pacy, lively, and happily free of the poetic diction which weighed down many of her first efforts. The discipline of writing children's verses (around five hundred in about two years) may well have helped her to continue or rekindle her interest in writing poetry.

Its next flowering took its occasion from *Phantasmion*, the fairy story which had its beginnings as an entertainment for her children,

13 See pp. 87–93.
14 Her diary entries for February to May 1834 make clear the extent of her wretchedness and prostration: 'I have scarce any hope of a recovery from my spiritual weakness' (27 February); 'O wretched wretched day! ... Today my feebleness and hysterical wretchedness is beyond all former misery. God alone can help and relieve me.' (3 March); 'Alas! I am more *completely* miserable I think than I have ever yet been' (7 May; HRC).
15 'The narrow Escape', p. 104.

but continued – again at her husband's urging – into a substantial story published by William Pickering in 1837. The plot is happily digressive and elaborate, too intricate to be summarised here – though I have given brief indications of plot and context before each of the songs. The first sentence of the book is arresting and extraordinary, and gives a good flavour of its character and method:

> A young boy hid himself from his nurse in sport, and strayed all alone in the garden of his father, a rich and mighty prince; he followed the bees from flower to flower, and wandered further than he had ever gone before, till he came to the hollow tree where they hived, and watched them entering their storehouses laden with the treasures they had collected; he lay upon the turf laughing and talking to himself, and, after a while, he plucked a long stiff blade of grass, and was about to thrust it in at the entrance of the hive, when a voice just audible above the murmur of the bees, cried 'Phantasmion!'

Like its protagonist, the story follows its wandering pleasure into scenes of enchantment. Phantasmion becomes a young man and faces various trials and ordeals before the wicked are vanquished and he arrives at a rather sombre version of a happy ending. Hartley Coleridge wrote some finely responsive lines in his copy of the book, referring to the story as:

> this waking dream
> This murmur of a distant stream –
> This shadow of a purple mist
> Of self-diffusing Amethyst –[16]

The songs from *Phantasmion* are all reprinted in this edition. As George Saintsbury remarked, 'most of the songs are in undertones. They have, however, an air of suppressed power'.[17]

Sara Coleridge Editing: Editing Sara Coleridge

'Our father never gave a thought to the arrangement of his poems' – thus Sara to Derwent on 24 January 1852. She and her brother were at the time giving the matter plenty of thought, working on a new

16 *New Poems*, ed. Earl Leslie Griggs (1942), p. 114.
17 *The Cambridge History of English Literature*, Volume XIV, (1915), p. 127.

edition of STC's poetry. This was the last of Sara's grand editorial efforts with Coleridge's *Nachlaß*, and she worked very hard on it in her last year, often writing to Derwent, her co-editor, twice a day. At the same time she was putting her own literary house in order, so her editorial principles have a bearing on how she wanted her own work to be read.

Coleridge left his poetic output in a colossal mess.[18] Hypertext might have been invented for him. Sara of course lacked this option, and in letters to Derwent she outlined some of her own principles for editing poetry. Most importantly, she preferred a chronological presentation to a thematic one. This was problematic with Coleridge – 'I am baffled in the attempt at *exact* chronology by the classes into which the "Sib Leaves" are thrown by Father, which *must* remain'[19] – but it was the principle on which she worked. Her argument was partly a psychological one: 'this alternation of grave and gay, light and heavy, sublime and humorous – is, to my mind, the very charm of a book of poetry'.[20] A chronological arrangement, moreover, bears with it a double historical interest, showing the unfolding of a poetic career both as a kind of intellectual autobiography, and as a history of the writer's response to his or her times. This edition, therefore, is ordered as far as possible chronologically according to dates of composition and publication;[21] and I am happy to echo Sara's 'Preface' to Coleridge's *Poems* (1852): 'the agreement with chronology in this Edition is approximate rather than perfect: yet in the majority of instances the date of each piece has been made out, and its place fixed accordingly'.[22]

Faced with the prolific and industrious chaos of her father's literary remains, Sara set about putting it in order. To do so was quite a family enterprise in the decades following Coleridge's death in 1834. Among his early editors we find Sara's cousin and husband Henry Nelson Coleridge and her brother Derwent, as well as Sara herself. There were many good reasons to edit his work: financial, for royalties; biographical, in that introductory materials could defend him against the damaging biographical studies that cashed in on his death, often under-informed or informed by malice; socio-political, moved by the

---

18 'The mess is the message', as Michael Neve once put it, apropos Coleridge. But it can't very well be for his editors.
19 To Derwent Coleridge, 27 January 1852 (HRC).
20 To Derwent Coleridge, 24 January 1852 (HRC).
21 These are detailed in the 'Notes on the Poems', pp. 212–42.
22 p. vii.

conviction that his thinking contributed in timely and valuable ways to the debates in early Victorian England; and psychological, especially for Sara, who had seen little of her father when a child. There is a sense in which her editorial work made a success out of her relation with him, and triumphed over the daughterly resentments discernible in her unfinished 'Autobiography'.[23] But it is possible to exaggerate these: she had moved to Hampstead on her marriage in 1829, and for the next five years she frequently saw her father in nearby Highgate, a neighbourliness which belies Virginia Woolf's romanticised idea that she 'found her father, in those blurred pages, as she had not found him in the flesh'.[24] Moreover, the psychological motivations behind her editorial work were not its only groundings; she was also moved by the impressive intellectual convictions which made her call herself 'a follower out of the principles of STC myself, whithersoever they lead me, because they seem to me the *very truth*'.[25]

'To Mr. W. and my father I owe my *thoughts* more than to all other men put together', she wrote on another occasion,[26] and the influence of such a father as Coleridge could not but be immense. But the parent with whom she spent most time was her mother, and in her poems maternal relations bulk larger than paternal ones. The titles of the two indispensable biographical studies of Sara give less than the full picture: Griggs's *Coleridge Fille* (1940) does not even allow her her full name, while Mudge's *Sara Coleridge: A Victorian Daughter* (1989) belies the fact that she was all of 35 when Victoria became Queen, and by that time was a Victorian mother of two. Her daughterly subjection was less than these titles suggest. In some respects the anxiety of influence was a greater burden for Hartley, also a man, also known to be a poet, than it was for Sara. One of Hartley's unpublished sonnets begins: 'Full well I know – my Friends – ye look on me / A living spectre of my Father dead – '.[27] At any rate, Sara was able to summon tones of moving forbearance, both towards her father and his adversaries, in her edition of *Biographia Literaria*: 'He who wrote those works wanted a "little here below" ere he went hence and was no more seen: he wanted a little encouragement from friends, a little fair play from adversaries, a little sympathy, and a little

---

23 Transcribed from manuscript in Bradford K. Mudge, *Sara Coleridge: A Victorian Daughter* (1989), pp. 249–66.
24 *The Death of the Moth* (1940), p. 115.
25 Letter to Justice Coleridge, July 1843, in *Memoir and Letters of Sara Coleridge*, ed. Edith Coleridge (1874), p. 202.
26 To Isabella Fenwick, 7 July 1847, in Edith Coleridge, *op. cit.*, p. 315.
27 Hartley Coleridge, *New Poems*, ed. Griggs, p. 69.

money'.[28] Her sympathy and her sense of grievance are controlled by the mildness of tone in this beautifully modulated sentence: its unclamorous evocation of a world of disappointment belongs to the same sensibility as her best poetry.

Virginia Woolf's essay on Sara Coleridge ends:

> she died at forty-eight, leaving, like her father, a blank page covered with dots, and two lines:
>
> > Father, no amaranths e'er shall wreathe my brow –
> > Enough that round thy grave they flourish now.[29]

Actually, she didn't. She left a 22-line poem, perhaps her best-known, of which these are the first two lines. And the second line, crucially, ends with a colon plus dash, not a full stop: the relationship to her father is a parenthesis in this first verse of the poem, not its final word. Its central subject is not her father, but her late husband. Moreover, Sara did not 'leave' the poem unfinished in the way she left the auto-biography unfinished, tailing off into a series of dots – (although not 'a blank page covered with dots', which would be showily defeated in a way Sara did not go in for). She completed the poem, which Woolf would have known from Griggs's biography, the book under review in her essay. She also dated it, which Woolf could not have known from Griggs – and indeed by placing the poem at the end of his chapter on Sara's editorial work, Griggs does give the misleading impression that she wrote it near to her own death in 1852. But she left more than one manuscript of this poem, including the one in the Red Book, where it is clearly dated 1845 – which is to say *before* she undertook her major editorial work, and not 'close to death', as Mudge suggests.[30] It is the first poem in the MS section headed 'Poems of Sara Coleridge in Widowhood', and its context is the death of her husband in 1843, lamented in passionately solemn tones reminding us that Sara's poetry was contemporary with Emily Bronte's:

> Father, no amaranths e'er shall wreathe my brow, –
> Enough that round thy grave they flourish now: –
> But Love 'mid my young locks his roses braided,
> And what cared I for flow'rs of deeper bloom?
> Those too seemed deathless – here they never faded,
> But, drenched and shattered, dropp'd into the tomb.

---

28 *Biographia Literaria* (1847), i. clxxiii.
29 *The Death of the Moth*, p. 118 (punctuated thus in Woolf). Sara was actually 49 when she died.
30 *Sara Coleridge: A Victorian Daughter*, p. 177.

The fleeting blooms here have a precursor in 'The Pair that will not meet' (p. 100). In both poems Sara is considering what might endow the world with the visionary gleam which Wordsworth described in his 'Immortality Ode'. 'To my Father' imagines that love can make its possessor careless of the laurels of fame, in which light Coleridge's poetic amaranths take second place to the requited marital love which he did not enjoy in his own life. 'The Pair that will not meet' imagines love outranking nature in lending a glory to the world, and thereby differs from Wordsworth's great ode:[31]

> My youthful compeer once was rosy Health
> She led me forth beside the sparkling rills;
> But Love by Fortune ruled came but by stealth,
> And while my feet were bounding o'er the hills
> This heart was heavy with a load of care;
> Mine eyes turned inward on a shadowed mind:
> That Lake was bright – but Henry was not there:
> In vain does Nature smile when Love's unkind.

'To my Father', then, cannot rightly be taken as evidence of Sara's resentment that her filial labours have choked her own creativity. More generally, indeed, the body of poetry in this edition stands as evidence that her literary life was in many ways happier, more fruitful and less spasmodic than we had thought. For instance, the Red Book includes several poems from the mid-1840s headed 'for *Phantasmion*'[32] (published in 1837), suggesting a creative continuity between these periods of her life, rather than a passing interest in the world of children's literature simply put by when her own children grew older. Moreover, two of these poems 'for *Phantasmion*' were included in the 78 pages of drafts for 'Howithorn' (1848) – the long inchoate balladic poem (unmentioned by both biographers) in which she re-explored the magical setting of *Phantasmion*, and returned with new intensity to themes of unrequited love and sexual disguise.[33] The edition gives some evidence that Sara continued to write poetry throughout her adult life, and that her critical and creative labours, though they jostled for priority, were far from incompatible.

---

31 Compare the early 'Epistle from Sara to her sister Mary whom she has never yet seen, her "Yarrow Unvisited"', in which she also implicitly takes issue with the Wordsworthian precursor.
32 See pp. 177–81 and 183–6.
33 For 'Howithorn', see Appendix, pp. 199–211, and 'Notes', pp. 242–5.

NOTE ON THE TEXT

For reasons given in the introduction, the poems are ordered chronologically, by date of publication when possible, and otherwise by date
of composition.

When the poem was published in Sara Coleridge's lifetime, the
published version has been used as copy-text. In other cases, I have
used the Red Book (RB) or the five volumes of Children's Verses
(CV) as copy-text; and used other manuscripts (MS) as copy-text only
for poems and drafts included in neither RB nor CV. In cases where
the poem exists in more than one version, I have made RB the copy-
text unless otherwise noted. The notes at the end give sources and
dates (in some cases conjectural) for all poems, and also give fuller
bibliographical details of the Red Book and the volumes of children's
verse.

The Red Book and CV poems are readily legible, while many of
the MS ones are difficult or impossible to decipher. I have put
doubtful readings in square brackets, for instance '[?sighed]', and the
very few indecipherable ones (on pp. 149 and 244–5) in square
brackets, with some indication of the number and length of the illegible words, for instance '[———— — —————]'.

The poems that Sara Coleridge saw through the press tend to be
more heavily punctuated than the fair copies she made in RB and
CV, and her manuscript drafts are the least punctuated of all. These
differences are preserved in this edition; the notes give sources for all
the poems. I have not altered or added to her punctuation, except in
a few cases to close quotation marks and provide full stops and question marks when these were clearly intended. It has sometimes been
impossible confidently to distinguish between her semicolons and
colons, and in a few cases between her commas and full stops, but I
have made my best guess for these and not recorded them in the text
or notes.

The text has been very lightly edited. I have modernised the layout
of quotation marks and parentheses, and the spelling of a few words
and usages (such as 'tis, not 't is, and hers not her's). I have expanded
Sara Coleridge's elisions, most frequently for past tenses ending 'd,
except in those cases where the elision helps to indicate the metric
(as in 'Heav'n' and 'flow'r', both of which she uses often).

For many poems Sara Coleridge recorded alternative words and
phrases – and in some cases lines and stanzas – above or between the
lines, or in the margins or at the end. Some of these look like second

thoughts or intended revisions, some of them alternatives between which she has not yet decided. I have not incorporated any of these alternatives into the text, on the grounds that when she clearly wanted to change a word or line, it has been deleted. But – although this is not a variorum edition – I have recorded the most substantial and interesting variants in the notes. Both here and in my inclusion of a few draft poems and scraps of light verse, I have tried to err on the side of preserving everything that looks as if it might be of interest, either as being good verse or as being illuminating about Sara Coleridge.

ABBREVIATIONS

MS   manuscript

HRC   Harry Ransom Humanities Research Center, where all the quoted manuscripts are housed unless otherwise noted.

People

DC   Derwent Coleridge (1800–83), the younger of SC's two surviving brothers

DMC   Derwent ('Derwy') Moultrie Coleridge (1828–80), son of DC and Mrs DC

Edith C   Edith Coleridge (1832–1911), SC's daughter

HC   Hartley Coleridge (1796–1849), SC's eldest brother

Herbert C Herbert Coleridge (1830–61), SC's son

HNC   Henry Nelson Coleridge (1798–1843), SC's first cousin and husband

Mrs DC   Mary Coleridge, née Pridham (1807–87), who married DC in 1827

Mrs STC Sarah Coleridge, née Fricker (1770–1845), SC's mother

SC   Sara Coleridge (1802–52)

STC   Samuel Taylor Coleridge (1772–1834), SC's father

Manuscripts

CV1   a small bound volume, 112 pages, uniform with CV2, CV3 and CV4, inscribed 'Herbert Coleridge. Volume I' on the front cover. The poem on its inside cover is dated 13 February 1834, and the book contains 58 poems, of which 33 were published in *Pretty Lessons in Verse*.

CV1a   a smaller, undated book, 72 pages, with a metal buckle on the front. It is undated, but of the same time as CV1. In a list of SC's children's poems in Edith C's hand it is called 'the 2nd vol'.

CV2   inscribed 'Feline Family. II' on the front cover. It includes 65 poems, of which one, 'Foolish Interference', is taken for *Pretty Lessons in Verse*. The poem on the inside cover is dated 19 April 1834.

CV3   inscribed 'The Kid. III' on the front cover. The book is dated 30 May 1834, and contains 26 poems, then two pages of chil-

dren's handwriting practice, a page of scribble, twelve blank
diary pages for the months of 1840, then five poems also found
in the Red Book, and a piece of light verse by Herbert dated
1847.

CV4   inscribed 'Latin. 4' on the front cover. A book of Latin grammar
and vocabulary exercises, including a single poem in English
('The Valley of Tempe was fair to the sight').

RB   the 'Red Book', a red leather-bound book with transcripts of 87
poems (five in Italian not included in this edition)

Books

DWL   *The Letters of William and Dorothy Wordsworth: The Early Years,
1787–1805*, ed. Ernest de Selincourt, revised by Chester L.
Shaver (1967)

EC   *Memoir and Letters of Sara Coleridge*, ed. Edith Coleridge (1874
single-volume edition)

Griggs   *Coleridge Fille: A Biography of Sara Coleridge*, by Earl Leslie Griggs
(1940)

Hainton   *The Unknown Coleridge: The Life and Times of Derwent Coleridge*,
by Raymonde Hainton and Godfrey Hainton (1996)

HCL   *Letters of Hartley Coleridge*, ed. Grace Griggs and Earl Leslie Griggs
(1941)

Mudge   *Sara Coleridge, a Victorian Daughter: Her Life and Essays*, by
Bradford Keyes Mudge (1989).

PL   *Pretty Lessons in Verse for Good Children* (1834)

STCL   *Collected Letters of Samuel Taylor Coleridge*, ed. Earl Leslie Griggs
(6 vols, 1956–1971)

Towle   *A Poet's Children: Hartley and Sara Coleridge*, by Eleanor A. Towle
(1912)

GUIDE TO FURTHER READING

Works by Sara Coleridge

Translations

An Account of the Abipones, an Equestrian People of Paraguay, from the Latin of Martin Dobrizhoffer (3 vols, 1822). Translated by Sara Coleridge. 'Preface', pp. [iii]–vii.

The Right Joyous and Pleasant History of the Facts, Tests, and Prowesses of the Chevalier Bayard (2 vols, 1825). Translated by Sara Coleridge. 'Preface', pp. v–xv.

Original works

Pretty Lessons in Verse for Good Children (1834). Fifth edition, 1853; reprinted 1927.

Phantasmion (1837). Reprinted 1874, with a preface by John Duke Coleridge; and 1994 (Woodstock Books), with an introduction by Jonathan Wordsworth.

Contributions to editions of Samuel Taylor Coleridge

S.T. Coleridge: *Aids to Reflection in the Formation of a Manly Character*, fifth edition (2 vols, 1843), ed. H.N. Coleridge. 'Essay on Rationalism' by SC, Vol. 2, pp. 335–556.

S.T. Coleridge: *Aids to Reflection in the Formation of a Manly Character*, sixth edition (2 vols, 1848). 'Essay on Rationalism', Vol. 2, pp. 13–248, and 'Extracts from a New Treatise on Regeneration' by SC, Vol. 2, pp. 249–322.

S.T. Coleridge: *Biographia Literaria*, second edition (2 vols, 1847), ed. H.N. Coleridge and Sara Coleridge. 'Introduction', pp. [v]–clxxxiv, and 'Biographical supplement', Vol. 2, pp. 311–447 (by HNC up to p. 390, then taken over by SC from pp. 391–447). There are also numerous essay-length notes, especially in Volume 2.

S.T. Coleridge: *Confessions of an Inquiring Spirit*, second edition (1849). 'Advertisement', p. [iii]; 'Note on Mr. Coleridge's Observation Upon the Gift of Tongues', pp. 221–30; and 'Examination of remarks contained in an article of the English Review entitled "Tendencies toward the Subversion of Faith", in the form of a Note on the "Confessions of an Inquiring Spirit"', by SC, pp. 231–89.

S.T. Coleridge: *Notes and Lectures upon Shakespeare* (2 vols, 1849).

'Advertisement', Vol. 1, pp. [v]–vi; 'Notes' to Vol. 1, pp. 337–72; 'Notes' to Vol. 2, pp. 363–71.

S.T. Coleridge: *Essays on His Own Times* (3 vols, 1850), ed. Sara Coleridge. 'Preface', Vol. 1, pp. xi–xvii, 'Introduction', Vol. 1, pp. xix–xciii, 'Notes' and 'Appendix', Vol. 3, pp. 999–1034.

S.T. Coleridge: *The Friend*, fifth edition (3 vols, 1850).

S.T. Coleridge: *The Poems of Samuel Taylor Coleridge* (1852), ed. Sara and Derwent Coleridge. 'Preface to the Present Edition', pp. [vii]–xiv.

S.T. Coleridge: *Notes, Theological, Political and Miscellaneous* (1853), ed. Derwent Coleridge. 'Note on Mr. Coleridge's Observation upon the Gift of Tongues. By Sara Coleridge', pp. 409–15.

Reviews

'Review of Tennyson's "The Princess, a Medley"', *Quarterly Review* 82 (March 1848), pp. 427–53.

'Review of Alexander Dyce's "The Works of Beaumont and Fletcher" and George Darley's "The Works of Beaumont and Fletcher"', *Quarterly Review* 83 (September 1848), pp. 377–418.

Writings published posthumously

Memoir and Letters of Sara Coleridge, ed. Edith Coleridge (2 vols, 1873); reprinted in one volume, 1874; one volume, abridged, 1875; one volume, 1973 (AMS).

Sara Coleridge and Henry Reed, ed. L.N. Broughton (1937). Includes SC's letters to Reed and her comments and marginalia on Gray and Wordsworth.

Bradford Mudge: *Sara Coleridge, a Victorian Daughter: Her Life and Essays* (1989). Includes eight essays by SC, pp. 187–266.

Main bibliographical and archival sources

Harry Ransom Humanities Research Center: University of Texas at Austin: the Coleridge Family papers include over 2,000 letters and numerous unpublished manuscripts by Sara Coleridge.

Victoria University Library in the University of Toronto: the Samuel Taylor Coleridge Collection.

Carl L. Grantz, *Letters of Sara Coleridge: A Calendar and Index to her Manuscript Correspondence in the University of Texas Library* (1968). University of Texas doctoral thesis describing the letters now housed at the Harry Ransom Center.

Biographical works and sources

Eleanor A. Towle: *A Poet's Children: Hartley and Sara Coleridge* (1912)

Earl Leslie Griggs: *Coleridge Fille: A Biography of Sara Coleridge* (1940)

Bradford Mudge: *Sara Coleridge, a Victorian Daughter: Her Life and Essays* (1989)

Kathleen Jones: *A Passionate Sisterhood: The Sisters, Wives and Daughters of the Lake Poets* (1997)

Dennis Low: *The Literary Protégées of the Lake Poets* (2006)

Minnow Amongst Tritons: Mrs S.T. Coleridge's Letters to Thomas Poole 1799–1834, ed. Stephen Potter (1934)

Letters of Hartley Coleridge, ed. Grace Griggs and Earl Leslie Griggs (1936)

The Letters of Sarah Hutchinson from 1800 to 1835, ed. Kathleen Coburn (1954)

Collected Letters of Samuel Taylor Coleridge, ed. Earl Leslie Griggs (6 vols, 1956–71)

Raymonde Hainton and Godfrey Hainton: *The Unknown Coleridge: The Life and Times of Derwent Coleridge* (1996)

COLLECTED POEMS OF
SARA COLERIDGE

EARLY POEMS 1815–1829

Valentine written in girlhood – perhaps at 13 years of age

O thou, who lov'st 'mid mystic groves to stray,
Eutorpe fairest of the sisters nine,
Sweet amatory Muse, inspire my lay,
Or lend that soul-entrancing lute of thine,
That I, with something of a fire divine,
May melt the frozen heart of her whom more
Than light or life I prize, than earthly thing adore.

Yes, lady, from those all too beauteous eyes
Resistless Cupid pierced my vanquished heart;
For these the cruel boy in ambush lies,
Triumphant whets his sanguinary dart,
And thence inflicts full many a bitter smart;
For ne'er, since Argive Helen's glorious day,
Hast thou ruled o'er mankind with such despotic sway.

For they do shine so very dazzling bright,
They may be likened to that wond'rous shield,
Which did so totally o'erpow'r the sight,
That those who looked on it straightway did yield,
And fell in deadly swoon upon the field:
But ah! their influence longer far doth last
Alas! it ne'er shall cease till life itself be past.

Those golden ringlets scarce less bright than they,
Impending o'er that forehead's purest snow,
'Mongst which the wanton Zephyrs lightly play,
Wafting them ever gently to and fro,
Into men's hearts sad harbingers of woe,
Are like the flag which heralds furious arms,
Less dang'rous far than thy sunbright celestial charms.

Lady, with gentle pity view my love,
Nor from my tender passion turn away,
Lest I the hapless fate of Clytie prove,
Wasted before thy beauty's potent ray,
Or like sad Iphis dead before thee lay,
And thou, like her he loved, repentant see,
And all too late to save bewail thy cruelty.

Translated from Horace in early youth

What graceful youth, on beds of roses laid,
Courts thee, O Pyrrha, in the pleasant shade
Of some rude cave, where gadding eglantine
The boughs with honeysuckle doth entwine?
For whom with simple neatness dost thou bind
Thy golden ringlets waving to the wind?
Alas! how oft with tears shall he deplore
Thy vows of faith – the Gods his friends no more!
And shall behold with terror and surprise
The ocean swell and the black tempest rise
Who now enjoys thy smiles and hopes to find
That thou art ever constant, ever kind.
Ignorant alas! of the deceitful gale
Causing him soon his folly to bewail.
How wretched they, caught in thy beauty's snare,
Who of thy faithlessness are unaware!
But just escaped from shipwreck on that sea
My dripping garments I have vowed to thee,
Tridented Neptune, pow'rful Ocean's God,
Who rul'st the roaring billows with thy rod.

Praises of a Country Life

How blest is he who far from Cares,
    Like the old race of Men
His own paternal fields doth till
    Free from all wrongful gain,

To action he is neither roused
    By the harsh Trumpet's sound
Nor trembles at the angry sea
    Which rages all around.

He either joins the fruitful vine
    To the tall Poplar Tree,
Or feeding in a shady vale
    His wand'ring flock doth see

Or cutting off the useless bough
    More healthy plants he rears
Or pours fresh honey into jars
    Or Sheep so tender shears

But when adorned with Apples sweet
    Glad Autumn lifts his head
How he rejoices in the Pears
    And in the Grape so red

With which, O Priapus, he thee
    Will bounteously reward
And thee, Sylvanus who doth well
    His territories guard.

Now in the shade he loves to lie
    Under the ancient Oak
And now upon the verdant grass
    Beneath th'o'erhanging rock

Meanwhile the dashing waters fall
    Birds in the forest sing
The little streamlets murmuring flow
    All which sweet slumbers bring.

But when the winter cold and bleak
   Loud storms of Snow prepares
He either drives with many dogs
   Fierce boars into the snares,

Or on a stake spreads slender nets
   The Thrushes to surprise
Catches the Cranes or timid Hare
   To him a joyful prize

Amongst these tranquil calm delights
   The country doth impart
We not the cares of Love forget
   Joyous and light the heart

But if at home a modest wife
   He hath, and children sweet
Like Sabine or Apulian Spouse
   That is so swift of feet

Who piles the wood upon the fire
   When he comes weary home
And pens the cattle in the field
   That they no more may roam

While from their teats abundant store
   Of sweet milk she doth steal
And bringing fresh wine from the cask
   Prepares a simple meal

No Lucrine Shell-fish Trout or Char
   Appears more sweet to me
If driv'n from th'east by thund'ring storms
   They e'er approach this sea

No Afric bird, or woodcock rare
   Do more my palate please
Than ripest Olives plucked from off
   The best boughs of the trees,

Or rhubarb that the meadows loves
　　Or mallows from the wood,
Or Lamb at Terminalian feast
　　Or kid, delicious food

The while, how pleased his sheep to see
　　All homeward hastening,
Or wearied oxen languidly
　　The heavy ploughshare bring;

And slaves that crowd the rich man's house
　　Day's labour being done
All circling round the cheerful fire
　　At setting of the sun […]

'I dolci colli, ov'io lasciai me stesso'

Those pleasant hills high towering into air,
Where lingers with delight my captive soul,
Are ever in mine eyes, and still I bear
Love's burthen even to earth's extremest pole.
Oft do I strive to free myself in vain
From the sad yoke imposed by despot Love:
Nor Time, nor Distance e'er relieve his pain
That's doomed such cruel woes as mine to prove.
Swift bounding o'er the plain the wretched hart,
Which cruel huntsman from afar espies,
Receives into his side the barbed dart
That pains him all the more, the more he flies; –
Thus rankling in my side Love's shaft doth lie,
'Tis death to tarry, but what pain to fly?

'Vago augelletto, che cantando vai'

Sweet little bird, that in such piteous strains
Dost sing, or rather mourn'st the fading year,
Seeing dark night approach, and winter drear,
While day and the gay months forsake the plains, –
Oh could'st thou know what kindred woes I bear,
By what resembling griefs my mind's opprest,
Thou sure would'st fly and hide thee in this breast
Thy dolorous laments with me to share.
Perhaps we have not equal cause to sigh; –
She whom thou mournest still may sojourn here,
While Fate has snapped my loved one's earthly tie!
But yet the grieving for the altered year
And thought of joys and sorrows long past by
Calls from mine eye the sympathetic tear!

Extract from an Epistle from Emma to Henry

When Heaven is filled with Cynthia's soothing light,
Around my couch thy form, as mildly bright,
No longer thwarted by the glare of day,
Sheds, moonbeam of my soul, its tender ray;
From Sleep's approach a soft enchantment gaining,
O'er Sleep itself with kindest influence reigning;
And, with the sun returning to the skies,
That constant image meets my waking eyes,
Rescues my soul from dull oblivious power
Or dreadful visions that around me lower,
And o'er this bosom reasserts its right,
Dear Contrast to the troublous forms of Night! –
Musing on that loved image thro' the day
Along my native Greta's banks I stray,
Gaze on the stream, and half unconscious hear –
Those rippling sounds that soothed my childish ear,
And gave with their calm undersong relief
To my full heart oppressed with joy or grief.
How sweetly does the lulling murmur seem
To mingle with my life's too cherished dream!
Yet Henry, when those eyes I first beheld,

Their burning glance my spirit almost quelled,
And, too intense, imparted to my mind
A nameless dread, – a feeling undefined; –
But now thy gentle heart I better know
'Tis but a warm yet soft and steady glow,
No wild unquiet fire, I fondly deem; –
Now gladly would I meet their cheering beam!
And oft I think how kindly, tenderly,
When last we parted, they were turned on me!
E'en now before me do I see thee stand
Invested with Affection's halo bland –
So vivid, so distinct seems to mine eyes
That shade, my heart it almost satisfies!
I scarce dare hope for greater happiness,
For joys more real in a world like this;
And when I dwell on Henry's raptured strain
I almost dread that we should meet again,
Lest closer ken the dear deceit remove,
And I less please, and he less warmly love.

Sometimes my thoughts o'er bitter fancies range!
I tell myself e'en Henry's heart may change; –
And then I pray that heaven will grant me power
To steel my spirit to that trying hour.
Yes! on some other he may bend those eyes
Once bent on me – breathe o'er again those sighs –
Tell her he never truly loved before,
Swear all those tender oaths to me he swore! –
All this by Emma may be shall be borne! –
Her Henry happy why should Emma mourn? –
Thus dream I – from that trance of breathless fears
Glad to be startled by my gushing tears.

To Elizabeth S.K. Poole

One bright May-day we've spent together,
One happy day of genial weather,
Ourselves in Life's delightful Spring! –
To celebrate with honour due
Our meeting blithe, our warm adieu,
I'd fain a vernal garland bring.

But Fancy's favours are not mine,
And all unused to deck her shrine
To call upon her name I fear! –
Her wreaths of more resplendent hue
The partial Nymph reserves for you,
For you, sweet Maid, her bright compeer!

Oh! would she aid one ardent prayer
Poured forth for you her favourite fair,
Content I'd end this farewell lay –
That still howe'er the seasons roll,
Her airy dreams may glad your soul,
There keeping up perpetual May!

To Zoe King

Zoe! When first I saw your face,
So exquisitely fair it seemed,
So full of still and silent grace,
That, gazing fixedly, I deemed
Some waxen image met my view,
No living child of human frame! –
For simple then I little knew
That Life and Zoe were the same.

Still seem, methinks, the ringlets fair,
Now that in riper years we meet,
The polished brow, the placid air,
To justify my fond conceit.
But ah! those eyes that softly move
Feelings of tenderest love to claim,
That voice, those livelier graces prove
That Life and Zoe are the same.

The air serene, the tranquil brow,
Bespeak a soul unvexed by strife; –
Long be the years, sweet maid, as now
With all that cheers, that breathes of life;
And when those mortal charms decline,
The vital spark of heavenly flame
Triumphant o'er the grave shall shine,
And Life and Zoe be the same.

To Edith May Southey during absence on the Lily of the Nile

Now Phoebus, dear Coz, gives all Nature to smile
    In this mountainous vale of our birth,
And your beautiful nursling, the Pride of the Nile,
    Again rears her form from the earth!

Ah, little we thought, when we marked the tear steal
    Down your cheek as you bade us adieu,
That its delicate bosom the plant should reveal
    Two summers unnoted by you!

Men tell you that form, so attractively fair,
    Appears in the Lily, portrayed, –
That the loveliest flower may be proud to compare
    With the white-armed and elegant maid, –

And I cannot but own the comparison just –
    How just I reflect with a sigh,
When I see your fair image return to the dust,
    And think all such beauties must die!

But yours is a soul that in purity vies
    With the exquisite flower we commend! –
A soul rich like that can with dignity rise,
    With graceful humility bend!

Ah! return with those charms to delight us, dear Maid,
    Nor continue forgetful to roam,
Content, as your rival to bloom in the shade,
    And spend all your sweetness at home!

[Valentine to Rose Lynn]

The Red Rose is a beauteous flower
Admired and loved where'er 'tis seen,
But not for shape or hue alone
The Red Rose is the Garden's Queen.

No, 'tis because her blushing leaves
With grateful odours fill the air,
Discoloured, dead yet fragrant still
Those leaves are treasured up with care.

Thou art a living, breathing Rose
Then be the Rose's sweetness thine
And still when time has faded thee
I'll be thy loving Valentine.

My dear dear Henry!

'Wad some Power the giftie gie you'
    To inspect each damsel's heart
Who for love alone is ready
    With her maiden name to part, –

Tho' they thicker be than flow'rets
    Which in May the meadow wears,
Not in one you'll find such true love
    As to you your Sara bears!

To the tune of 'When icicles hang by the wall'

When fires wax dim and chimnies growl,
And tea and toast no more go round,
And sits mine host like solemn owl,
And Mirth lies snoring on the ground
Beneath the dining-table laid,
And folks 'gin cry with sleepy head
      'O dear!
What shall we do?' – a drowsy note, –
Then read or say these rhymes by rote.

When cards nor music show their power,
Nor, best of all, the light quadrille,
'To dispossess the present hour,'
And jog old Time against his will; –
When puzzles e'en are heard with glee,
And folks begin to cry, 'Bless me!
      O dear!
What can it be?' – a tedious note, –
Then read or say these rhymes by rote.

Sequel

Henry
Did you say it to insult me, Miss? and do you think it probable
That where *I* am things can come to such a pass? –
It would seem that instead of by far the most agreeable
Of Flirters and Small-talkers I were some stupid ass!

Without further preface, Miss, I'd have you to know
That music is not *dreamt* about when I choose to be witty,
And no girl cares to trip it on the light fantastic toe,
When I sit beside her, and tell her that she's pretty.

Sara
Indeed, my dear Henry, I haven't the least doubt of it;
'Tis a fact which I'm sure I've no reason to deny;
But ere you leap adown the ditch, be sure you can get out of it;
Know that hearts may be lost in the twinkling of an eye!

Besides you must learn soon to bid these airy toys adieu,
Nor play the gay Lothario all the days of your life;
Do but think when Hymen catches you, and throws his hempen
                                              chain round you,
What scores you'll have to pay when he binds you to a wife!

'Let it not a Lover pique'

Let it not a Lover pique
To have German for his Greek;
Since whatever tongue they speak,
Kisses tender once a week,
Pressed for him by maiden meek,
(Oft so called in phrases sleek)
Should be well received by her man,
Even tho' they babble German!

'How now, dear suspicious Lover!'

How now, dear suspicious Lover!
(Doubts and jealousies all over!)
Send unkissed an empty blank,
So to make thee waste thy kisses,
Like an April fool, – and thank
Faithless one for unsent blisses!
No, my loved one! – three times three
(Oft as bee the nectar sips,)
Was this circle pressed by me!
Cordial may it prove to thee,
For my heart was on my lips!

Laugh not, you easy Sylphs! as you hover in the air,
To see me press so tenderly the paper's pallid cheek!
Why letters may not learn to kiss, I pray you to declare,
For 'tis a well known fact that they long since have learnt to speak.

'Now to bed will I fly,'

Now to bed will I fly,
And hope there to lie
In comfort and quiet; –
So please not to riot
On my wretched face,
You detestable race,
Whose infamous name
I'm forbid to proclaim;
(Tho' I think it all Fudge,
An implacable judge,
For I owe them a grudge;)
Gnats, midges or fleas,
(Call them whate'er you please)
Their actions declare
That they certainly are
No better than those
Ignoblest of foes,
Who valour do lack
To make the attack
In open daylight; –
So stealing by night,
To murder will creep
The innocent sleep; –
My recent assailants
Are such sorry gallants.
By this morning's light,
The field of the fight
(I mean my poor face,)
Proved them equally base; –
Then I vow in Hate's name,
Whoever may blame,
Since as Bugs they behave
The *name* they shall have; –
For who handsome does,
To make no more fuss,
Handsome *is* by my fay!
And vice versa!
This metaphor leaving,
To another now cleaving, –
The day after a feast,
Tho' last, is not least;

Nay, some think it best,
When plenty remaining
To stop all complaining,
The savory treat
We hungrily eat
With comfort and glee
Sans cérémonie.
Now I earnestly hope
The gourmands who grope
Thro guilt, sheet and blanket
At my cost to banquet
Think not in this fashion
But have moderation,
Nor mean to renew,
Insatiable crew!
Their revellings too –
Their gluttonous theft,
Of conscience bereft,
On that which is left
From last night's debauch,
Which alas! is not much!
In this case I wot
Must pay scot and lot;
And therefore most humbly their plundered host begs,
They'll consider there's reason in roasting of eggs!

'They tell me that my eye is dim, my cheek is lily pale,'

They tell me that my eye is dim, my cheek is lily pale,
They look to hear me heave the sigh and see me sadly weep; –
Yet while my Henry lives and loves, I nothing seem to ail,
But think of him the livelong day, and thinking fall asleep!

No heavy grief lies on my heart and chills the life-blood there,
No starting tear have I to check that scarce will be represt; –
I'm happy as a bird that carols in the air
And knoweth well she is not far from her own loved nest.

Yet surely, after all, these fading looks of mine
Must in some sort come from the absence of my dear!
While I read his tender words I were thankless to repine,
And yet I cannot choose but say, 'O would that he were here!'

How can the eye look bright when it roves about in vain
And never never lights upon the one beloved face?
How can the glowing rose on the widowed cheek remain,
When Hope and Memory only that blissful sight replace?

Go, you may call it madness, folly — &c.

Go! You may call me dowdy, tabby,
I will not cast old clothes away!
There's such a charm in going shabby,
I would not, if I could, be gay!

O! had you felt the satisfaction
Of causing money far to go,
You'd own the secret sweet attraction
Some folks are too rich to know!

'O! once again good night!'

O! once again good night!
And be thy slumbers light,
Pleasant thy dreams and bright
        As sun-clad mist; —
And when they disappear,
O! may thy mind be clear
From every doubt and fear,
        As lake by breezes kist!

'Art thou too at this hour awake,'

Art thou too at this hour awake,
Or musing thus sink'st thou to rest?
Dost thou of these dear thoughts partake
That fill thy Sara's faithful breast, –

While one loved image casts a spell
O'er all her soul's entranced powers,
Possesses – charms her but too well,
And steals from sleep the silent hours? –

O! wherefore ask? – Hast thou not sworn
Thy gentle heart is mine to hold? –
Ne'er will I doubt – ne'er can I mourn
Hopeless until that heart grow cold.

Do what thou wilt! – glad homage pay
Right eloquent at Beauty's throne –
Thou wilt not cast my love away,
Nor pierce a bosom all thy own.

Now on my knees – till morning light
I'll pray high Heaven to shield from harm,
And guard from perils of the night
My Henry with protecting arm!

Sweet be his sleep! – and if he dream,
O! may his visions soft and bright
Show like the Moon's reflected beam
In some calm lake on summer night!

To Louisa and Emma Powles

For courtesies and kindnesses
　　And sundry obligations
Of gentle looks and pleasant words
　　And frank communications, –
For service to my Album done
　　With pen and eke with pencil
Some fit return I long to make
　　By means of each utensil.

Within this book – (had I the skill,
　　I'd make no vain resistance)
Pleased would I give some fruit or flower
　　A long and bright existence!
Or paint, perchance, a worthier task,
　　In colours richly glowing,
That sister pair of blossoms fair
　　To whom my thanks are owing!

A worthier task! – but mine alas!
　　A hand nor strong nor steady;
And better painters than myself
　　Have done that work already.
The best of wishes, gentle friends!
　　Are all I have to offer, –
O! for Urganda's magic power!
　　'Twere then a noble proffer.

A friend of yours and mine maintains
　　Howe'er the point we carry,
Our sexes' earnest wish and dream
　　Is, first and last, to marry!
Be this the truth, or slander base,
　　Whate'er the Fates may send you,
In single or in wedded life
　　Good luck, dear Maids, attend you!

May Luisita's speaking eyes
    Ne'er tell of long-felt sadness,
Ne'er overflow except with tears
    Of tenderest, holiest gladness!
And since her charms, her poet swears,
    To Earth than Heaven are nearer
For this ev'n, to an earthly Lord
    May she but prove the dearer!

For Emma – (not e'en pictured babes
    More purity and sweetness!)
Hers be the joys of pensive souls
    In all their blessed completeness!
Hers be the rosy thoughts of youth
    Unmixed with thorns of sorrow,
The fairy Castles in the air
    Renewed on every morrow!

May each succeeding Fancy prove
    A bright and blithe new comer,
And when her buoyant Spring of life
    Is changed to richest Summer
And maiden liberty resigned
    For love and kind protection,
O! may she yearly more and more
    Rejoice in that election!

'Yes! With fond eye my Henry will peruse'

Yes! with fond eye my Henry will peruse
Verse where no gems of Wit and Fancy shine; –
Doth Love inspire – needs not Parnassian Muse
To please a heart which he has sealed for mine!

I have not sought to place my dullard lays
In Albums gay the glittering leaves between,
Where each coy poet lies in wait for praise,
And lurking hopes he shall not lurk unseen.

One eye indulgent may they some day meet,
Albeit read in works of higher skill –
May one kind gentle heart responsive beat,
Nor scan the verse, but love the writer still!

Naught heeds yon peasant all the vernal quire,
The rich wild carol and the liquid tone;
Yet lists complacent, by his cottage fire,
To one poor bird that pipes for him alone.

'"How swift is a thought of the mind"'

'How swift is a thought of the mind'
    When winged both by Fancy and Love!
Three hundred long miles left behind
    The Robin's caressed by the Dove!

But if to bills more within reach
    The Robin his faithless beak joins,
Not with kisses, but pecks will she teach,
    And this severe penance enjoins.

Whatever gay bird he may see,
    Howe'er she his fancy may suit,
No homage of eye must there be,
    His flattering tongue must be mute.

He shall not tell the pheasant or jay
    How brilliant their plumy attire;
Not a word to the lark shall he say,
    But in silence her strains must admire.

He shall not praise the shape of the swan
    The most graceful of all waterfowl,
But till six months are over and gone,
    Must pass for an old stupid owl!

Verses to my Beloved with an empty purse

Matter 'tis of pleasant thought,
While my fingers swiftly run,
That for him the purse is wrought,
Who so long my heart hath won!
He will deign the gift to bear!
He will deem it passing fair!

Soft the silk thy Sara weaves
For thy service and delight,
Softer than the velvet leaves
Of the pansy richly dight,
Like a little Queen of old
All in violet and gold! −

Softer than the moss that clings
On the rocks by Derwent's river,
Or the down of Cupid's wings,
His the boy with bow and quiver,
Or the feathers of the dove,
Or thy heart, my gentle Love! −

Softer than young Hylas' beard,
Or Diana's bashful cheek,
Or the strains in woodland heard,
Strains so melancholy meek,
What time Cynthia gives her light,
Goddess excellently bright!

Softer than the wild duck's nest,
Or the peacock's purple neck,
Or the halcyon's plumy vest
Which all radiant hues bedeck!
Softer than the cygnet's breast
By the circling waves carest, −

Or the pulp of melting peach,
Or the baby panther's skin,
Or the young leaves of the beech
When first peeps their tender green,
Or the sea-nymph's streaming locks
Which she dries upon the rocks! −

Softer than the dust that lies
In the foxglove's speckled bell,
Or the tear in Laura's eyes
Springing up from Pity's well,
Or her bosom gently heaving
While her inmost soul is grieving, –

Or the snow-drift lightly pressed,
While the wintry blasts are sobbin',
To thy chill and trembling breast,
O thou fond and gentle Robin!
Or the fleecy summer cloud
Chased by Zephyr piping loud, –

Or the fruit whose lusciousness
Oft my Henry would compare
With the lips he loved to press
Of the Maid he called so fair,
Or his accents sweetly speaking –
Such the silk I have been seeking!

Finer never silk-worm span,
And the colour brightest crimson!
Not the gorgeous ottoman,
Which a Sultan lays his limbs on,
Is with richer silk bespread!
Such a deep and glowing red,

When a summer evening closes,
Tinges all the western sky;
Such those oriental roses
Which the attar scent supply,
Or Aurora's dewy fingers
While within the East she lingers!

Such the hue thy cheek assumes,
Modest Maiden blushing bright!
Such the hue of Robin's plumes
Like my Henry's face of light,
Or the wound in my poor heart
When from him I sadly part!

Crimson is the tint of Joy,
Rosy red Love's proper hue!
Fitter could I not employ
When I weave a purse for you,
You all other joys above!
You my best, my only Love!

Many a ripe and luscious fruit
Glowing in the western isles,
Many a shell and stone and root,
Hidden deep from Phœbus' smiles,
Might in colour likened be
To the purse I weave for thee!

Just so red the ruby wall,
Shedding radiance most divine,
Of Apollo's flaming Hall!
Just so red the mantling wine
Raised aloft in tipsy wassels!
Such this purse adorned with tassels,

Closed by circlets scarce less fair
Than the ring that thou must give me,
When to Hymen thou shalt swear
For thy helpmate to receive me! –
Every ornament thus vaunting
What can such a purse be wanting?

What it wants I shall not name,
Leaving that to shrewd surmise,
'Tis the charm I cannot claim
In my partial Henry's eyes!
'Tis the only good we miss
To complete our perfect bliss!

Were it mine, I need not send
Thus with aching, longing heart
Tokens to my distant friend,
But with him would take my part,
With anticipating zeal
Studying what he would reveal!

Now no more! – this tedious strain
Far too long, I fear, has lasted!
Sure my Henry will complain
Of his time and patience wasted,
And have cause enough to curse
Both the poet and the purse!

'My Henry, like a modest youth,'

My Henry, like a modest youth,
    Avows his kisses are not sweet,
But if he told the honest truth,
    He'd own he thinks them quite a treat!

As good he oft has said before,
    And vowed, whatever I might say,
That our coy sex loved even more
    Than th'other did this sort of play.

Meek creature sure I must have been
    Ere to forgive this heinous speech!
How could those lips a kiss e'er win,
    When such the doctrine they dared preach!

And if they be not sweet, good Sir,
    Why bid me to so base a feast?
A courteous host would sure demur
    To serve a dish unsweet at least!

Oft have I been by you accused
    Of a propensity to angling,
Whene'er a modest phrase I used,
    Which made us straightway fall a-wrangling; –

You must confess that you surpass
    Your mistress in this worthy art,
Yet now you're catching weeds and grass,
    (I mean an answer dry and tart;)

Instead of slippery eel or trout,
　　The meet reward of such good fishing,
Or shining char or turbot stout,
　　The compliment for which you're wishing!

Am I on such a theme as this
　　To flatter any saucy youth,
To say he give a honied kiss
　　With nectar lips? – not I forsooth!

To please an angler so complete
　　Must I deny his words are true,
And say his mouth is far more sweet
　　Than full-blown roses bathed in dew?

No! thus much only will I say
　　Which without bait he might have caught,
That be his lips whate'er they may,
　　To me they are with sweetness fraught!

No other pair beneath the Moon
　　To me are either sweet or dear; –
I ceased to view them all too soon –
　　O! were their owner ever near!

To Mrs Whitbread

Her eyes are still bright and as joyously beaming
As if they were strangers to fast flowing tears;
Luxuriantly still her dark tresses are streaming
As they played on her neck in Life's earliest years!

The rose, that with pleasure she views brightly glowing
On her loved one's young cheek, has not fled from her own;
Her form all the graces of Hebe is showing,
Her voice tells of Youth in its gladdening tone!

O! how can the owner of charms such as these
'Mid our heath-covered mountains have sojourned so long?
O! how can seclusion and solitude please
One who might be the gaze and delight of a throng!

'Tis the fond mother's heart that with tenderness swelling
Has bid her repair to our lone little vale;
For Innocence sure in such vales must be dwelling,
And Health seems to breathe in the fresh mountain gale!

'Tis the spirit delighted for ever to dwell
On all that is fair in earth, water and sky, –
To list to the tale which sweet Nature can tell,
To gaze on her charms with poetical eye!

'Tis a heart and a soul formed to love and admire,
That have caused her a sojourner here to remain,
And the sight she is leaving a wish will inspire
To visit our heath-covered mountains again!

'O, how, Love, must I fill'

O, how, Love, must I fill
This dreary, dreary blank –
How do your eyes no ill,
Yet fully use my frank? –

By putting there a token
Of what you called a bliss,
When tender words were spoken –
When you asked me for a kiss!

'When this you see'

When this you see
May those dear eyes
Be clear and free
As Summer skies!

When this you read
May that kind heart
No solace need,
Feel no sad smart!

When this you close,
Believe it penned
By one who glows,
Best, dearest friend,
With love for you!
In haste, Adieu!

'"I am wreathing a garland for wintry hours",'

'I am wreathing a garland for wintry hours',
    Thus whispered a Youth to his mistress the Dove,
'The verses you pen are the sweetest of flowers,
    Their fragrance delights me – it breathes so of Love!'

'Yourself is the Sun whose warm radiance divine
    Gave life to those flowers', cried the fond little Dove;
'Their incense will rise while that Sun deigns to shine,
    They never can wither while cheered by your Love!'

'Henry comes! No sweeter music'

Henry comes! No sweeter music
    Ever strikes upon my ear
Than his dear advancing footstep,
    Which I sit and long to hear!

Henry comes! From toil returning,
    Sick of gloom and worldly strife,
O! let peace and joy attend him
    In the presence of a wife!

Hence then every bitter feeling!
    Hence each low and sordid care!
Let my thoughts be pure and gentle
    Fit for him I love to share!

Let my soul be fresh and bounding
    As the merry mountain brook,
Cheering him with tons of gladness,
    Yielding to his earnest look!

Like that clear transparent streamlet,
    All its liquid depths unclose,
And like that a faithful mirror
    Which his soul, reflecting, shows!

To Susan Patteson with a purse

Green and Gold and Violet,
Fair and well-commingled hues,
Ev'n as in a rainbow met,
Such the colours that I choose
In the silken purse to weave,
Gift that Susan will receive.

Green and Violet and Gold –
Such the colours that appear
On Mount Skiddaw's bosom bold,
When the air is fresh and clear,
By the glowing light of day
In the merry month of May!

Larches of the tenderest green
Fit for Spring's transparent vest,
Heath-clad rocks that peep between
All in roseate Purple drest,
Golden Furze around them clinging
On the air sweet odours flinging, –

All of these are softly blended
On my native mountain now; –
Would that ere the Summer's ended
Thou could'st climb its lofty brow,
Or when vernal tints give place
To rich Autumn's mellow face!

'

Th'enamoured Nymph, whose faithful voice'

Th'enamoured Nymph, whose faithful voice
    Her loved Narcissus' words repeated,
Was sure a type of Henry's choice,
    Tho' he nor vain nor self-conceited!

Each kiss he sends with kindness winning
    She echoes by a kiss as fond; –
Nature prevents her from beginning,
    But lets her sweetly correspond.

Three hundred miles too intervene,
    And maiden modesty relieve,
The blushes ne'er by Henry seen
    She trusts her lover will conceive.

Epistle from Sara to her sister Mary whom she has never yet seen, her 'Yarrow Unvisited'

Now, Mary, Winter's reign suspended,
    Our mountains doff their hoods of snow;
Rich purple hues of heath are blended
    With green, and furze's golden glow.
Yon Lake, whose name thy Derwent bears,
    No more of darkish steely hue,
Now glitters silver bright, now wears
    The heaven's reflected sapphire blue.

Attended by the frolic Wind
    Sweet Spring each field and grove attires,
Yet holly-berries still remind
    Of frost and snow and Christmas fires.
The foliage of the chestnut droops
    Like Naiad's drenched and clinging robe;
Aurelians bloom in yellow groups,
    And half unfold the tiny globe.

I hail the burnished celandine,
    That ever to my childish eye
The Sun's low emblem seemed to shine,
    And told a tale of Summer nigh;
And bright the crimson leaves are gleaming
    Of many an infant sycamore,
Most like, to playful Fancy's seeming,
    The roof of some gay fairy bower.

In russet weed no longer drest,
    With which 'gainst wintry winds she strove,
The Beech-tree dons her vernal vest
    To match the livery of the grove;
And hers the Lime now 'gins to wear,
    Summer's own light and summery tree,
The tardy Ash alone stands bare,
    And tells of beauty yet to be.

How many Springs have bloomed and faded,
    Since one whose name thou lov'st to hear,
On Greta's bank with trees o'er shaded
    Joined in my sports, a pleased compeer!
Nature and all her stores were new,
    Nor then of coming care and strife
Distressful presages I drew, –
    A brother's love illumed my life.

Mary, 'twere sweet but long to tell
    How dear thy Derwent was to me,
By knoll and wood and rocky dell
    How blithe we wandered, fancy-free! –
How o'er the stream to safe dry land
    His sylph-like sister oft he bore,
And guided her with gentlest hand
    Thro' flowery fields of classic lore!

A winsome playmate then had we
    Who climbed the trees with vaunted skill, –
No lily statelier now than she
    Presiding in the gay quadrille: –
Now seen 'mid tricksy crowds to shine,
    Fashion's admired and graceful child,
Then like the breeze-fanned eglantine
    She danced and gambolled sweetly wild.

How oft we wont in Winter days
    On Greta's frozen stream to play,
Or toil the stone-piled bridge to raise
    By one light shower soon swept away;
Or weave in Summer's balmy hours
    Fresh garlands on the river's brim,
Or spoil the banks of choicest flowers
    Transplanted soon to gardens trim!

Since then, where Greta's waters glide
    How often have I wept and mourned,
Summer in all her blooming pride
    And Nature's bounty almost scorned!
These scenes in loveliness arrayed,
    While tears and sorrow still were mine,
In their calm beauty did upbraid
    A soul that could not but repine.

I thought of one so fondly deemed
    The child of Genius and of Worth,
By thoughtless follies unredeemed,
    Low laid upon the soiling earth;
While Friendship many a bitter tear
    Sheds o'er the wreck of time mis-spent,
And Hope grows sick, and will not hear
    The promise e'er so truly meant.

Oft as I wandered forth to pray,
    And saw the elm-tree's lace-like vest
Grown black to mourn th'expiring day
    Athwart the wannish-silver West, –
I imaged brighter skies than ours,
    The tropic land in all its wealth
Of giant trees and gorgeous flowers,
    Where Henry sought the treasure health!

Not smoother ran my true-love's stream
    Than mountain brook by rocks impeded,
Tho' here and there the sunny gleam,
    The tranquil flow have been conceded; –
Yet when each random light was fled,
    And Care had ta'en me for his mate,
Tears too for Derwent's sake I shed
    And mourned my brother's wayward fate.

Immersed in gloom and misty tears
    His life's horizon seems to lie, –
No hope, no joy my bosom cheers
    When thitherward I bend my eye; –
But soon the darkness and the storm
    Seem chased away by magic sleight;
My Spirit sees an angel form
    Arising bathe the scene in light!

Mary! – I ne'er beheld thy face,
    And cold and vain description's art
A breathing portraiture to trace,
    Such as can satisfy the heart: –
Thine eyes the colour of thy hair,
    Each feature told me o'er and o'er,
I know them all, how sweet, how fair –
    Methinks a sister should know more!

Oft when my spirit lies enthralled
  Neath Morpheus' wild fantastic sway,
Our future meeting is forestalled
  I view thee who art far away!
But Sleep, delighted to distress,
  Each dream of thee with sadness taints,
And, ere the vision vanishes,
  Mars all that waking Fancy paints.

The liveliest image of thy mind
  I see in lines thyself hath traced;
These show thee tender and refined,
  With purity and meekness graced: –
In these the welcome warranty
  Of deeply cherished hope I view,
That thou and I may live to be
  Dear friends, affectionate and true!

How oft in thought from hills sublime
  That now my farthest prospect bound,
I'm carried to a softer clime
  And one sweet plot of cultured ground!
I see the borders flower-besprent,
  The modest lilies round them wreathing,
The years, an ancient monument,
  Where all things else of Youth are breathing!

Rose-trees, their buds yet scantly seen,
  Snow-drops, whose blossoms all are shed,
The inner garden's leafy screen, –
  The prospect far below outspread: –
I see a face known long ago,
  Which faithful Memory hath portrayed,
And one that still I only know
  By Fancy's blest pictorial aid!

When She depicts the future scene,
  And Hope imparts her glowing hues,
A sister's gently-beaming mien
  The picture with delight imbues.
Mary! these visions of my own,
  All sweet and soothing as they be,
O! may I change, ere weary grown,
  For truth and blest reality.

'The Rose of Love my Henry sends,'

The Rose of Love my Henry sends,
  Seems to my heart bright hues to wear,
And balmy fragrance it dispends
  That dissipates each brooding care.

How can it sweetest odours shed –
  How can it bloom so fresh and fair –
How can its leaflets gaily spread,
  While we are still a severed pair? –

Fold up thy leaves, thou bonny Rose,
  And hide thee from the rifling air!
Those precious odours fast inclose,
  Nor let rough blasts thy vesture tear!

Planted in Hymen's happy soil,
  And tended by a blessed pair,
Those beauties thou shalt soon uncoil,
  And scatter all thy fragrance there!

''Mid blooming fields I daily rove'

'Mid blooming fields I daily rove
  By Greta's dashing stream,
Or where thro' calm sequestered grove
  The Lake's blue waters gleam.
I watch the spruce and jocund year
  Her gay attire still changing; –
Sweet Nature to my soul is dear
  While 'mid her works I'm ranging.

But blooming fields are not so sweet
  As Henry's blessed presence!
His look of love, whene'er we meet,
  Of Joy contains the essence.
No lake that gleams twixt ivied trees
  Is half so bright and cheery
As thy bright eyes, whene'er they please
  To shine on me, my deary!

How can I bear no more to view
   Glad Nature's smiling features –
To bid these lovely scenes adieu,
   The lonely wand'rer's teachers!
A thousand times more dear to me
   My Henry's loving heart,
Than all the charms mine eye can see,
   From which I fain would part.

The dashing Stream is not so clear,
   So soothing and refreshing
As that dear voice I love to hear,
   All tender thoughts expressing.
From flowers and trees and purling brooks
   How gladly would I sever,
To dwell 'mid smoke and pent up nooks
   In Henry's presence ever!

'Those parched lips I'd rather press'

Those parched lips I'd rather press
   Than richest fruit, that brightly glowing
Hangs in tempting lusciousness,
   Where the genial gales are blowing!

I'd rather sit from hour to hour
   Lulling thy griefs and cares to rest,
Than lie in soft Arcadian bower
   By Zephyrs fanned, with roses drest!

I'd rather hold that hand in mine,
   And watch my Henry's languid eye,
Than like a ballroom beauty shine
   'Mid song and dance and revelry.

Sickness

Elastic May, with all the jocund train
Of Summer months, and Autumn bright and clear,
Move on apace, and leave me wasting here –
Not one of them with soft breath lulls my pain: –
The Sun that like a giant runs his race,
The Stars which mortal weakness ne'er assails,
And Cynthia whose fixed visit never fails,
Fair image of a young health-radiant face –
Swift meteors, shooting stars, and rainbows fine,
Whose blended lines glad village girls may wear
At merry-makings in the open air,
While Nature's rival colours round them shine –
These I have ceased to view, and O 'tis well!
Since I am faultering, sinking on my way,
The sight of Nature, ever young and gay,
Might lead my tutored spirit to rebel.
Yet those bright shews are now of higher worth,
Summoned by Thought and gorgeously combined,
Than when I moved unfettered as the wind –
They help to build for me new Heav'ns and Earth,
For as a Mountain, rising in the West,
Appears transfigured by the Sun's past light,
And, while the shades are gathering, looks more bright
Than late it seemed, in noon-tide splendour drest,
So the unconquered mind, by suffering tried,
For which few pleasures and few hopes remain,
Some exquisite delights e'en yet may gain,
That in Life's gladder season are denied.

Written in my Illness at Hampstead during Edith's Infancy

I've heard of some whose genial forces fail,
Victims of sickness, wasting slow and sure,
Who ne'er again shall meet the joyous gale,
Ne'er bound o'er springy turf with step secure.

Yet these can smile, or if a tear they shed,
It cools the 'fever of the languid heart', –
Gay hope and joy – Life's fragrance – all are fled,
And they resigned and almost pleased to part.

While Pain relenting leaves them doubly calm.
Or Fever paints the vivid glowing dream,
O'er aching brows Affection sheds her balm,
And lovely forms from Memory's mansion stream.

No gloom is theirs, while clothed in Heav'n's own light
Yon Lake upholds her liquid mirror near;
For them the trees and flow'rs are blooming bright,
The woodland quire for them is echoing clear.

The world recedes, but patient Faith has made
An inner world to which their soul conforms –
They loved the sunshine, but can brook the shade,
Glad to find shelter from careering storms.

The keen regret to feel that now no more
They act in busy scenes their strenuous part
Is past away – life's task not wholly o'er, –
To suffer bravely satisfies the heart.

The ruddy cheek, the gay and sparkling eye,
Their vigorous neighbour's mien with health elate,
Spreads sunshine o'er the breast, that heaves no sigh,
Nor heeds the contrast to their own estate.

They love the flow'rs by friendly hands enwreathed –
Ah! never more to wander where they grow!
Some cheerful tale in gentlest accents breathed,
Can light in faded cheeks a transient glow.

Their steadfast fancy by no fears opprest
Reveals a soothing vision to their sight;
They see a grassy grave with daisies drest
And bathed in heav'nly beams of cheering light: —

A grave, the image of that perfect rest
Which he who promised surely will bestow —
Sunbeams that tell them of those mansions blest
Whither th' ecstatic spirit longs to go.

Verses written in sickness 1833, before the Birth of Berkeley and Florence

My babe unborn, I dream of thee,
    Foreshaping all thy looks and wiles,
But Heaven's light may close on me,
Ere I thy real face can see
    Ere I can watch thy dawning smiles.

My older children round my heart
    For many a day have been entwined:
Yet dear to me, e'en now, thou art;
Fain would I do a Mother's part
    Ere life and love are both resigned.

You will not droop, my precious dears,
    When I am numbered with the dead:
You ne'er can know my cares and fears;
Your eyes will fill with childish tears,
    Which o'er my grave will not be shed.

When others weep and mourn for me
    That I no longer must be here,
Ne'er may they quench your childish glee;
No sadness ever may you see
    To check the laugh of thoughtless cheer.

But when you gain reflection's dow'r
   O ne'er thus joyless may you pine!
Ne'er may you know the anguished hour,
The sickening fears that overpower
   This crushed but struggling heart of mine.

In dreams an airy course I take
   And seem my tedious couch to fly:
Or o'er the bosom of the lake
Ere to captivity I wake,
   My skimming boat I swiftly ply.

But nought my waking hours can bless –
   I strive to sweeten Sorrow's cup;
'Tis all in vain, for ne'ertheless
I find it dregged with bitterness,
   When to my lips I lift it up.

My griefs are not to be expressed:
   Affection's voice can charm no more:
I ne'er shall find a steady rest,
Till, torn from all I love the best,
   I seek the distant unknown shore.

To Herbert Coleridge. Feb 13 1834

This little Book, my darling boy,
I well may dedicate to thee:
The verse was framed for thy delight
For thy bright eyes alone to see.

My hand is weak, beloved child
But I will use my hand for thee:
To write what thy dear tongue shall speak
That pleasure still is left to me.

My head's confused, my thoughts are dull,
But simple rhymes I still may find:
I'm all unfit for serious themes,
Yet may I please thy childish mind.

My heart, dear child, is often sad,
But thou shalt laugh with mirth and glee
At quaint conceits which I'll devise;
Sweet music is thy voice to me.

And though my dazzled eyes are dim
These letters I delight to trace,
To see my little Herbert read
With sparkling eye and glowing face.

Then darling boy accept the book
Which thus I dedicate to thee:
'Tis all thy mother now can do
For him she loves so tenderly.

Benoni. Dedication

My Herbert, yet thou hast not learnt to prize
   Parental love, that hovers o'er thee still;
   No heavy hours hast thou – no sorrows fill
Thy childish bosom when thou hear'st my sighs;
But thy fresh cheeks and pretty gleaming eyes
   Thy careless mirth, bring happiness to me;
   No anxious pitying love I ask of thee –
Be thoughtless still while swift thy childhood flies.
Hereafter thou, my Herbert, wilt discern
   With tender thoughtfulness this heart of mine,
That asked no present love, no full return;
And then, while youthful hopes within thee burn,
   Mayst dream that one to whom thy thoughts incline,
   E'en so may love some cherished child of thine!

The Months

January brings the snow,
Makes our feet and fingers glow.

February brings the rain,
Thaws the frozen lake again.

March brings breezes loud and shrill,
Stirs the dancing daffodil.

April brings the primrose sweet,
Scatters daisies at our feet.

May brings flocks of pretty lambs,
Skipping by their fleecy dams.

June brings tulips, lilies, roses,
Fills the children's hands with posies.

Hot July brings cooling showers,
Apricots and gillyflowers.

August brings the sheaves of corn,
Then the harvest home is borne.

Warm September brings the fruit,
Sportsmen then begin to shoot.

Fresh October brings the pheasant,
Then to gather nuts is pleasant.

Dull November brings the blast,
Then the leaves are whirling fast.

Chill December brings the sleet,
Blazing fire, and Christmas treat.

Trees

The Oak is called the king of trees,
The Aspen quivers in the breeze,
The Poplar grows up straight and tall,
The Peach-tree spreads along the wall,
The Sycamore gives pleasant shade,
The Willow droops in watery glade,
The Fir-tree useful timber gives,
The Beech amid the Forest lives.

What Makes a Noise

The Cataract dashing
　　Down over the rocks,
Comes foaming and splashing,
　　With furious shocks,
As loud as the crashing
　　Of thunder on high,
When lightning is flashing
　　Aloft in the sky.

The Nightingale

In April comes the Nightingale,
　　That sings when day's departed;
The poets call her Philomel,
　　And vow she's broken-hearted.

To them her soft, sweet, ling'ring note,
　　Is like the sound of sorrow;
But some aver, no need hath she
　　The voice of grief to borrow.

No, 'tis the merry Nightingale,
　　Her pipe is clear and thrilling;
No anxious care, no keen regret,
　　Her little breast is filling.

She grieves when boys have robbed her nest,
    But so would Stork or Starling;
What mother would not weep and cry
    To lose her precious darling.

Foolish Interference

The Caracal★ see, high up in the tree,
    The Lion beneath him is dining;
But, gorged with his prey, he marches away,
    The relics to others resigning.

The Caracal now jumps down from the bough,
    For blood is to him an elixir;
The gristle he gnaws, the tail and the paws,
    And every bone he doth lick, Sir.

A Barbary Ape gets into a scrape,
    By coming a little too near him;
'Twas very unsafe the creature to chafe,
    Yet thus did he venture to jeer him.

Says he, 'I am sure I ne'er could endure
    To feed at the board of a patron;
And second-hand meat I never would eat,
    Though hunting might cost me a great run.'

The Caracal stares, and frightfully glares;
    Says he, 'What you mention is true, Sir;
The thing you suggest shall soon be redrest,
    I'll make a fresh meal upon you, Sir!'

With this he turns round, and soon with a bound
    Is perched on the animal's back, Sir;
His blood he doth sup, he gobbles him up;
    The Monkey pays dear for his clack, Sir.

★ 'A sort of lynx that follows the lion, like the jackal' (SC's note).

Fine Names for Fine Things

The Sun is called Phœbus, the Moon is called Phœbe,
In Poems which Herbert will read very soon;
A bright blooming damsel is often called Hebe,
And Cynthia, too, is a name for the Moon.

The Seasons

Winter is a dreary time;
Then we hear the howling blast,
Then the trees are bare as hop-poles,
Rain and hail fall thick and fast.

Winter is a social season;
Then we gather round the fire;
Books and pictures then delight us,
Fun and feasting mirth inspire.

Spring's a variable season;
First comes zephyr mild and meek,
Then the east wind nips the blossom,
Sun and show'r play hide and seek.

Spring's a sweet and merry season;
Spring with garlands decks the thorn,
Fills the groves with songs of joyance,
Then the lamb and colt are born.

Summer is a sultry time;
Then the glare of light oppresses;
Lilacs fall, and gay laburnum
Parts with all her golden tresses.

Summer's a delightful season;
Then we view the gorgeous flowers,
Fragrant scents are wafted to us
While we sit in shady bowers.

Autumn time is melancholy;
    Then the Winter storms are nigh;
'Mid the garden's failing relics
    Mournful gusts are heard to sigh.

Autumn's a luxuriant season;
    Then the harvest glads our sight,
Fruits grow ripe; and, glittering pheasants,
    You must fall for our delight.

The Squirrel

Ay, there's the Squirrel perched aloft,
    That active little rover;
See how he whisks his busy tail,
    Which shadows him all over;
Now rapid as a ray of light
    He darts up yon tall beech;
He skips along from branch to branch;
    And now the top can reach.

Now view him seated on the bough
    To crack his nuts at ease,
While Blackbirds sing and Stockdoves coo
    Amid the neighbouring trees;
The light wind lifts his silky hair,
    So long and loosely flowing;
His quick ear catches every sound –
    How brisk he looks and knowing.

With cunning glance he casts around
    His merry sparkling eye,
In yonder Hazel by the brook
    Rich clusters can he spy;
His lofty station soon he quits
    To seize the milky store;
You ne'er can catch him, dearest child,
    The useless chace give o'er.

The Butterfly you once surprised,
  And had him in your power,
While he his painted wings displayed
  Upon the passion-flower;
As in the Fox-glove's bell he dived
  You caught the Humble Bee,
Examined well his velvet coat,
  Then gave him liberty.

With Lambkins you might run a race
  Though swift they hied away,
The nimble Kid attempt to chase
  Along the healthy brae:
But little Squirrel's more alert
  Than Butterfly or Bee,
No Lamb or Kid is half so light,
  So swift of foot as he.

The fleet Gazelle, the mountain Roe,
  You may not hope to seize,
And fruitless were it to pursue
  A leaf whirled by the breeze.
A Dolphin 'neath the ocean wave
  You scarcely could surprise,
Nor on the desert sands o'ertake
  The Ostrich as she flies.

Poppies

The Poppies blooming all around
  My Herbert loves to see;
Some pearly white, some dark as night,
  Some red as cramasie:

He loves their colours fresh and fine,
  As fair as fair may be;
But little does my darling know
  How good they are to me.

He views their clust'ring petals gay,
    And shakes their nut-brown seeds;
But they to him are nothing more
    Than other brilliant weeds.

O! how shouldst thou, with beaming brow,
    With eye and cheek so bright,
Know aught of that gay blossom's power,
    Or sorrows of the night?

When poor Mama long restless lies,
    She drinks the poppy's juice;
That liquor soon can close her eyes,
    And slumber soft produce:

O then my sweet, my happy boy
    Will thank the Poppy-flower,
Which brings the sleep to dear Mama,
    At midnight's darksome hour.

The Usurping Bird

A poor little toadie lived under a stone,
With nettles o'ershadowed, with lichens o'ergrown;
A Wheat-ear, of covetous spirit possest,
Resolved to obtain the snug hole for his nest.

Said he, 'Shall an animal, squalid and squat,
Inhabit this cozy desirable grot;
While I and my wife must ramble and roam,
To find a fit place for our nursery home?'

So saying, by dint of hard scratches and pecks,
And doing his utmost to harry and vex,
He forced the poor toad to abandon his cell,
And entered therein with his partner to dwell.

A warm little nest in this cave to construct,
The long trailing stems and dry glasses they plucked;
They lined it with feathers, with wool and with hair,
Which furzes from wandering animals tear.

Six delicate eggs of a soft bluish white,
The couple soon viewed with unmingled delight;
'My dear', said the father, 'that day will be blest,
When first our young Wheat-ears take wing from the nest'.

One morn he went forth, and was hopping hard by,
Intending his wife's noon-day meal to supply;
A feast he expected, the snails seemed so rife,
When down came the harrier, and ended his life.

For many an hour did his poor hungry mate
Her spouse's return with impatience await;
He never came back for her wants to provide;
Of sorrow and famine, poor birdie! she died.

Her relics were gnawed by the carrion crow,
And flies in the cave did the maggots bestow;
The eggs which the pair had so anxiously cherished
Were sucked by the magpies – or otherwise perished.

And thus was the grotto restored to the toad,
Who gladly hopped back to his former abode;
In safety dwelt he, for so livid a fright
Was even disdained by the hunger-starved kite.

Now this you may learn both from rhymers and preachers,
'Tis wicked to injure the meanest of creatures;
Tyrannical tempers we all should control,
Nor even expel an old Toad from his hole.

Edith Asleep

Fast, fast asleep my Edith lies,
　　With her snowy night-dress on;
Closed are now her sparkling eyes;
　　All her merry thoughts are gone.
Gone! ah no! perhaps she dreams;
Perhaps she views the crystal streams,
Wanders in the grove and field, –
What hath sleep to her revealed?

Bat and owl enjoy the night;
　　All the stars are sweetly twinkling;
While the Moon doth shed her light
　　On the brooklet gently tinkling:
Perhaps for her the Sun doth shine;
Perhaps she pulls the king-cups fine;
Merry birds around her singing,
Now she hears the echoes ringing!

Perhaps she bends beside the river,
　　Plucks aurelian's yellow globe,
Sees the willows wave and quiver;
　　Ah! she wets her fairy robe!
Where the water lilies float
Perhaps she guides the skimming boat,
Now the tender petals crushing,
Now the reedy thicket brushing.

Perhaps along the devious dell
　　She in fancy now may ramble,
Seeking moss or budding bell
　　Underneath the gorse and bramble.
Perhaps she's playing with the fawn
Up and down the grassy lawn;
Or with little lambkins skipping,
Or along the birch-grove tripping.

Perhaps she gazes on the pool
　'Neath the rock's black shadow lying;
From the mountain's summit cool
　Silvery distant lakes descrying.
Perhaps adown the rugged steeps
With the dancing rill she leaps;
See, her cheek begins to flush;
O, she's waking! hush! hush! hush!

The Blessing of Health

If ever my child were confined to a bed,
With limbs full of pain, and a dull heavy head,
　O how he would think of the days
When, lightsome and free, like a bird on the wing,
O'er upland or dell he was able to spring,
　On river and green-wood to gaze!

To breathe the fresh air underneath the blue skies,
Is worth all the cordials that med'cine supplies;
　My darling would prize it in vain;
O how he would long o'er the daisies to tread,
To leave the down pillows so carefully spread,
　And bound in the meadows again!

'In this dull apartment', he'd sadly exclaim,
'Spring, summer and autumn, to me are the same;
　In vain do the violets blow;
I never can climb to the heather-bell's bed,
Nor watch the rooks building high over my head,
　Nor glide where the water-flow'rs grow'.

To those that have health every season is sweet:
Hot Summer has flowers, and a shady retreat,
　Where thrushes and turtle-doves sing;
And lovely as light is the roseate glow
Which rests at bright dawn on the summits of snow,
　And dear is the promise of Spring.

And they that have never known sickness and grief
Admire the deep red or the light yellow leaf,
    Which soon shall be whirled from the bough.
Then Herbert, my child, to the meadows repair,
Make hay while it shines, and enjoy the fresh air,
    Till age sets his seal on your brow.

The Humming-Birds

A Marsh-bred Toad, intent to shun
The fervours of a tropic sin,
Entered a blooming arborous bower,
Where hung suspended from a flower
The Collibree – that plumed sprite,
Who takes his name from locks of light.
Words cannot paint the varied rays
Which on that elfin's frontlet blaze;
The pendent plumes that formed his tail
Wave in the scarcely breathing gale,
More exquisitely light and rare
Than beard of corn or maiden hair;
While topazes with rubies blent.
Rich lustre to his raiment lent.
Sir Toad, who, though a harmless creature,
Possessed no very handsome feature,
Struck with dire envy at the sight
Of that gay, glancing, glittering sprite,
Now seemed by contrast doubly curst,
Possessed of every creature's worst.
No brother cramped beneath the harrow,
No birdling tortured by an arrow,
E'er felt such pangs as this poor Toad,
Through envy's dart – dejection's load;
While heaved with sighs his leathern breast,
He thus his rankling grief exprest:
'O Nature, why hast thou conferred
Such splendour on a useless bird?
Why dost thou prodigally shower
Thy gifts on shell, and plant, and flower –
To me, to me alone, denied

The bloom of youth and beauty's pride?'
But see, what glances like a star,
A spangle shot from Luna's car!
No eye could tell from whence it came,
'Tis quivering like a lambent flame
In breezy air: it settles now,
With azure crown upon its brow,
That glances loveliest purple light;
A robe with glittering tissue dight,
Where emeralds into sapphires play,
To form a jeweled rainbow gay;
And stomacher of purest sheen,
Bedropped with eyes of golden green.
Behold the beamy sylph alight
Beside that ruby-vested sprite,
Who swelled with anger at the view,
And shrieked aloud, 'Hence, goblin blue!
A thousand blossoms round us glow,
In one of these thy form bestow,
But this datura's spotless shrine
To earthly bird I'll ne'er resign'.
'Fierce, fiery fright!' the sparkler screamed,
'If twice ten thousand blossoms gleamed
Within my reach, I'd ne'er retreat,
Through fear a mortal foe to meet.
Wert thou the eagle, paltry elf,
I'd bid thee fly, or guard thyself!'
The ruffled plumes, erected crest,
And swelling throat, their wrath exprest.
Can tiniest birds such passions know?
Does fire in downy bosoms glow?
In fight the fairy foes engage,
They dart their bills in deadly rage;
Those bills, as keen as tempered steel,
Give wounds no living wight can heal;
And rivulets of blood must flow,
To stain the fair datura's snow;
For triumph, not for her they die,
As breathless on her breast they lie;
While death itself but feebly tames
The splendour of those fairy frames.
Sir Toad beheld the dire event
With less of sorrow than content;

'Fine feathers make fine birds', cried he,
'Superior sense is left to me;
I'd ne'er consent to shed my blood,
For all the treasures of the mud'.
The heart that sinks and inly pines
Because another brighter shines,
Is sure within its depths to hide
Vain-glorious thoughts and sullen pride;
E'en Pity's self is chilled to death,
When touched by Envy's baleful breath.

Childish Tears

Childish tears are like the dew,
When bright day is fresh and new,
With the Sun's first kindly beam
Vanishing in subtile steam –
Leaving every bell and blade
Fresher, brighter, fairer made.

Thus when simple childhood grieves,
Simplest remedy relieves;
Touched by pleasure's gladdening ray,
Sorrow vanishes away,
While th'elastic spirits soar
Higher even than before.

Tears that fall from older eyes
From a deeper source arise;
When those bitter waters flow
May my child his Saviour know –
May he find the best relief
For the worst of earthly grief!

Man was made to mourn and weep,
Doomed the fruits of toil to reap;
When my child has learnt the truth
Of his heritage of ruth,
May he humbly, meekly pray,
'Jesus, wipe my tears away!

Teach my heart a worthier sorrow;
Strength and comfort let me borrow
For the bitter strife within –
Strife of weakness and of sin;
Gracious Master, make me prize
Happiness beyond the skies!'

Providence

Entwined amid fresh springing grass
    Doth odorous thyme her sweets exhale;
Those spicy leaves the flock will pass
    On scentless herbage to regale;

While bees, that with the faintest streak
    Of early dawn the fields explore,
Will that rejected nectar seek,
    And revel in the balmy store.

The Maker and the Lord of all,
    Who gives to men their daily bread –
Who marks each little sparrow's fall,
    And watches o'er the infant's head;

Great God, who bids the waves retreat –
    Who made the sky, the earth, and sea –
Spreads for the flock his pasture sweet,
    And guards the portion of the bee.

All these their Maker's law fulfil;
    By Nature led, they cannot stray:
But we, with choice of good and ill,
    Must learn to take the better way.

'Nox *is the night*'

Nox is the night,
　　When up in the sky
The bright twinkling stars
　　And moon you may spy.

Nux is a nut
　　Which grows on a tree;
By cracking the shell
　　The kernel you see.

Nix is the snow
　　Which covers the ground,
When trees have no leaves,
　　And flowers are not found.

'*A father's brother, mother's brother, are not called the same*'

A father's brother, mother's brother, are not called the same
In Latin, though an uncle is the only English name;
For *patruus* the first is called, from *pater*, I suppose;
The second is *avunculus*, as every scholar knows.
One kind of aunt is *patrua*, *avuncula* the other;
Privignus is a son-in-law, *noverca*'s a stepmother.
A grandmother is *avia*, and *nepos* a grandson;
And *avus* is a grandfather; – your task is not yet done.

　　Proǎvus means a great-grandfather;
　　　　Abǎvus, I have been told,
　　Means a man's grandfather's grandfather,
　　　　Who must be wondrously old.

　　Atǎvus – he is no lad,
　　　　He's a great grandfather's grandfather,
　　Tritǎvus means the grand-dad
　　　　Of a man's grandfather's grandfather.

The Celandine

'Are these the buttercups so gay
I thought they bloomed in merry May
Beside the fragrant clover?'
No, these are celandines, my child;
This March the weather is so mild
They stud the fields all over.

The buttercups unlike to them
Are raised upon a lofty stem
And seem to stare about them:
The celandines are lowly flowers
In early Springtime they are ours,
We scarce could do without them.

Perchance they think the daisy meek
When earth is chill and suns are weak
Should have some friend to cheer her;
And so before the meads are fine
Beside her bed the celandine
Doth make a sunshine near her.

'January is the first month in the year'

1

January is the first month in the year
When the weather is cold and clear:
Boys roll the snowball round and round
Or slide on the pond where the ice is sound.

2

February Fill-ditch then sets in
With a pelting rain that will wet you to the skin
Soon as the sky shews a speck of blue
How the pretty snowdrops gleam to view.

3

March comes on with wind from the East,
A wind good neither for man nor beast:
The daffodil flaunts it in yellow and green
What cares she if the wind be keen?

4

April's showers and sunshine bright
Paint the rainbow to our sight:
Then the violet smelling sweet
Under every hedge we meet.

5

May hangs blossoms on the thorn –
Then the lamb and colt are born:
Primroses forsaken die
Gaudier flowers engage the eye.

6

June with tulips, eglantine
Will be finest of the fine:
Rose and lily odours yield
New-made hay scents many a field.

7

In July the sultry night
Scarce will cool the weary wight:
Then the woolly sheep are shorn
Then the harvest home is borne.

8

August brings the juicy grape
Melons too of goodly shape:
Then the melting peaches come
Nectarine apple pear and plum.

9

In September hares must die
Grouse and partridge swift and shy:
Then's the time to hunt and shoot
Then's the time to gather fruit.

10

In October drink good ale
Soon the year begins to fail:
Drink the ale so fine and mellow
Though the leaves are turning yellow.

11

Chill November's surly blast
Tears the boughs and drives them fast:
Then the sleet mixed up with rain
Makes us of the wet complain.

12

Cold December's frosty air
Makes us to the fire repair:
Then good friends each other meet
To enjoy a Christmas treat.

The End.

'January brings the blast,'

January brings the blast,
Hail storms obscure the sky;
Lake and stream are frozen fast;
O'er the ice the skaters fly;
When the winds are gone to rest
Crumbs to pretty Robins throw;
See his soft and ruddy breast
Pillowed on a tuft of snow.

February veiled in clouds
Fills the pool and floods the plain:
Thickest mist the landscape shrowds,
Loosed is every icy chain:
When the sun is faintly beaming
We the golden crocus hail,
While the snowdrops softly gleaming
Shiver in the chilly gale.

Like a lion March comes in,
Ere his going we rejoice,
See the larches robed in green;
Hear the lively chiffchaff's voice;
Hark the breeze is sharp and shrill!
Sowers go to scatter seed;
Celandine and daffodil
With the daisy deck the mead.

April changing every hour
Paints the rainbow in the sky:
Then the bee is in the flow'r
Swallows then are sailing by.
Chaunts at eve the nightingale;
Cuckoo shouts from many a tree;
Primroses and cowslips pale
Bloom o'er every knoll and lea.

May hangs blossoms on the thorn;
Flora then puts on her pride:
Then the flock is washed and shorn,
Cygnets down the river glide.
Then rathe Primrose dies forsaken:
Then the busy turtle sings:
Shepherd boys glad Echo waken;
Fledgelings try their tender wings.

June brings crowds of blushing roses:
New made hay scents many a field;
Heav'n its deepest blue discloses,
Banks the richest odours yields;
Then the cherry blushes brightly:
Little rills are growing dry:
Starry glow-worms glitter nightly;
Butterflies with tulips vie.

In July the sultry hours
Make us seek the sheltered glade;
Honeysuckle, gillyflowers
Shed their fragrance in the shade;
Peonies in flaming knots
Grow beneath the Guernsey rose;
Mellow then are apricots
'Mid the corn the poppy glows.

August brings abundant riches,
Brings the pear and balmy plum,
Nect'rines glow beside the peaches
Then the swelling melons come:
Reapers o'er the sickle bend;
May their task be finished soon!
May no heavy show'r descend
Ere they view the harvest moon!

In September scared by man
Partridges from stubble fly;
Black-cock, grouse and ptarmigan,
Soon 'twill be your turn to die.
Tow'rd the end of mild September
All the fading flowers decline:
We the vintage may remember
While we sip the sparkling wine.

In October bright and clear
Huntsmen love the fox to follow,
Love to chase the flying deer,
Hart and hind with whoop and hollo;
Then the russet medlar's ripe;
Then to gather nuts is pleasant;
Sportsmen shoot the slender snipe,
Woodcocks and the shining pheasant.

Bleak November's sullen sky
Winter's gloomy reign confesses;
Gusty winds relentlessly
Tear the forest's yellow tresses;
Then the air is cold and hazy,
Filled with fog and blinding sleet;
E'en the little simple daisy
Blooms no longer at our feet.

In December we make merry,
Christmas time brings mirth to all;
Holly boughs with scarlet berry
Gaily shine upon the wall.
Then with rosy cups o'erflowing
Let us speed the parting year:
Hope within our bosoms glowing
Hail the future banish fear.

'Little Sister Edith now'

Little Sister Edith now
Eats her biscuit powder soon,
Milk brought from the gentlest cow
Nurse will give her with a spoon:
Once I was a baby too
And had neither bread nor meat,
Now I have got teeth to chew,
Many kinds of food to eat.

Little Sister Edith dear
Soon must have her bonnet on,
See the sky looks bright and clear,
All the darksome clouds are gone:
Nurse will carry sister sweet
Till her legs grow stout and strong,
Then with her nice little feet
By herself she'll trot along:

Once I was a baby too,
Not a single word could say,
I believe it very true,
That I could not jump and play:
Now my tongue can freely talk,
I can even learn to read,
I can run and dance and walk,
This has been a change indeed.

Sister's bonnet's made of straw
And the ribbons are of silk,
Brighter blue I never saw,
But her dress is white as milk.
I have got a hat to wear,
Bonnets are but girlish toys,
Petticoats I soon may spare
Trowsers are the thing for boys.

'Why those tears my little treasure'

Why those tears my little treasure
Why that sad and piercing cry?
Yours should be a life of pleasure
Sorrow's coming by and by.

Care will come and steal your roses
Grief may dim your sparkling eye,
Ere your light in darkness closes
You may feel as sad as I.

Could you see the clouds impending
O'er the scene so lightsome now,
See yourself in sickness bending
Frustrate every anxious vow:

Then your sighing weeping sobbing
Might have reason like my own:
Now your tears from me are robbing
Every joy that is not flown.

Those bright smiles my only pleasure
Those glad tones my only stay,
Joyous looks my greatest treasure
Steal not cruelly away.

Sad experience, strong foreboding
Make me shudder when you cry;
Anxious thought my bosom loading
Lest you e'er should feel as I.

Sara Coleridge for Herbert and Edith. April 19th 1834

Ten months I ministered my Herbert's food,
And gladly deemed that task should be renewed
For thee my babe, but weakness laid me low
And dried that fount and bade mine eyes o'erflow
With fruitless tears that on thy couch I shed,
And wished them pearls to crown thy precious head.
Too soon I felt, dear babes with twofold pain
My weakened limbs no more could yours sustain:
A mother's love can never change or die
Yet sometimes gazes with a heavy eye.
Partaking of the body's sore distress
It lives for sorrow not for happiness.
This chiefest sorrow my affliction knew
That suffering stole so many thoughts from you.
And this my comfort that your jocund eyes
Viewed tears in mine with no unblest surprise:
For what of tears can your light bosoms deem
But April gems that freshen where they gleam?
How have I longed to lead your childish feet
By mossy brooks to copses fresh and sweet!
That bliss denied this happiness I know
To point where blossoms of Parnassus grow
And garlands twine upon my sickly bed
To grace your pensive brows when I am dead.

Eye has not seen nor can the heart of man conceive the blessedness of Heaven

In sylvan shades where light can never dawn
The streamlet issues from its darksome cave,
Gleams a brief space along the forest lawn,
Then rolls in deepest gloom its dusky wave.

Anon it leaves for aye the tufted brake,
Its current now by rocks no more represt,
And spreading into yon resplendent Lake
Receives all Heav'n into its tranquil breast.

Thus human love in sorrow and in gloom
Awhile must wander on its earthly way,
But issuing from the shadows of the tomb
Shall beam at last in Heav'n's eternal day.

Divinest Charity that here below
Dispensed her draughts with care from scantiest brooks,
And sought the tender herbs and flow'rs that grow
Beneath sharp thorns amid the tangled nooks,

Shall there behold the endless streams of bliss
That glittering roll along their affluent tide,
And amaranthine blooms of happiness
In vast profusion heaped on every side.

And rapt Devotion that from earth's low sphere
Gazed upward with a steadfast fervent eye,
And ev'n where clouds and veiling mist appear
Discerned the Sun of promise in the sky:

Freed from the weaknesses of earthly mould
Shall dwell aloft ethereal and sublime,
The Sun of Righteousness for aye behold
Veiled by no cloud in Heav'n's refulgent clime.

Consolation in Trouble

'In Heav'n we all shall meet again!' –
Thus fancy soothes the sufferer's pain,
When anguish doth the bosom rive
And hearts against their sorrow strive,
And think it never can be true
That they for aye must bid adieu.

Your path, dear child, is ever bright,
You live in warm affection's light:
But think, though still your joys remain,
Think of that hour of bitterest pain
When mourning friends such sorrow know
They almost 'long themselves to go'.

O try to think of Jesus now
While dewy roses crown your brow;
O try to think of that blest place
Where you shall meet him face to face:
And while this earth is beaming fair
O think of brighter regions there.

Then when the hand that none can stay
Has torn your heart's best joys away,
When all the treasures of the earth
Seem to your fancy nothing worth,
This world a cloudy vale appears
To eyes that swim in briny tears.

Not long in grief you'll pine and mope
Like one that is bereft of hope,
Nor find it hard to look on high
With strange and unaccustomed eye,
Nor shrink desponding from the view
And think that heav'n's no place for you.

The friend who from your love is torn,
For whom not comfortless you mourn
You'll image there in blessed rest;
Your pray'rs so long to God addrest
That this dear friend might Heav'n obtain
You'll trust were not poured forth in vain.

That Saviour whom in buoyant youth
You sought in spirit and in truth
His Holy Comforter will send
A most beloved and well known friend;
His blest Redemption then will seem
A joyous but familiar theme.

The means of grace, the hope of glory,
A stirring though an oft told story
Will bring a succour to your grief
Better than creeping time's relief;
And you who long before had striven
To be not all unfit for Heav'n,
May think with mitigated pain
That there you'll meet your friend again.

Silence and attention at Church

O hushed my child be every idle word,
At church we must be ever mute and still;
Great wonders and glad tidings may be heard
Our minds with awe and thankfulness to fill.

Hear of that God who made earth, sea, and skies,
All that we view so excellent and fair,
Who spread the plains and made the mountains rise
And planted every flow'r that blossoms there.

Hear of his only Son, Redeemer blest,
Who left his throne of happiness and love
And sought a world of suffering and unrest
That we might dwell with him in realms above.

His tears were shed that we might weep no more,
His blood was given our sinful souls to save,
A heavy burden for our ease he bore,
And died that we might overcome the grave.

Then while such wondrous tidings may be heard
Try to forget your books, your work, your play:
Seek but to understand God's Holy Word,
And think to whom it is you kneel and pray.

'Grief's heavy hand hath swayed the lute;'

Grief's heavy hand hath swayed the lute;
      'Tis henceforth mute:
Or utters but a jangling strain
Which forces Echo to complain.
Though Pleasure woo, the strings no more respond
      To touches light as fond,
Benumbed as if by some Enchanter's wand.

Do thou brace up each slackened chord,
        Almighty Lord!
That which thou madest O restore,
And jocund as of yore
The Lute shall pour thanksgiving melodies
        On every breeze,
Strains that celestial choristers may please.

The Little Invalid

''Twere better to lie in a grave than a bed',
Thus poor little Henry his mother addrest;
'The spirit's anxieties then would be fled,
And then would the body be really at rest.
But now, when I'm free from the terrible pain,
My heart feels its bitterness worse than before,
To think that I'm banished from meadow and plain,
And never can sport with my playfellows more'.

'Yes, Pain and Privation stern visages wear,
And well', said Mamma, 'may my darling appal;
But aye for their presence our hearts to prepare
A mild-looking Maiden attends within call.
She'll soothe every pang, your disquiets allay,
And shew you a damsel all beaming and bright:
For Patience has never gone far on her way
Ere Hope follows fast from the mansions of light.

'*Her* voice is enchantment: she bids you espy
A glimmer of light on the shadiest bourne:
And when, pointing upward, she looks to the sky,
Her face kindles bright as a midsummer morn.
Yes Patience and Hope have rich blessings in store,
But ere they can enter our couch to attend,
Firm Faith in the Saviour must open the door,
And Faith, if we pray, will the Comforter send.

'Our passport to bliss by the Saviour ensured,
They render us fit in his sight to appear:
His infinite Goodness those Graces procured; –
They bless and support us while sojourning here.
They'll wipe all the tears from my precious one's eyes:
No more for lost pleasures he'll eagerly crave:
But e'en in his bed cherish time as it flies: –
Then may he with comfort look on to the grave'.

The mansion of Peace

Let him who would dwell in a mansion of Peace
Secure the foundations on Fortitude's rock:
For ne'er will this world's warring elements cease:
No building on earth is exempt from the shock.

'My friends in vain you chide my tears'

My friends in vain you chide my tears
From founts unknown to you they flow:
Thou Lord alone can'st count my fears,
The weight of my affliction know.

I ask Thee not to dry mine eyes
While here in Sorrow's world I dwell:
But O command their streams to rise
From blest Repentance' deepest well!

O strike this heart by grief congealed,
Which beams of love could never melt:
When to that touch it once shall yield
Grief's numbing hand shall be unfelt.

Then then these tears that daily rush
As if my very heart to drown
Will seem too tardily to gush
Too scantily to trickle down.

Ne'er shall I pray the streams may cease
Till deeper floods on floods arise
Do Thou but smile on their increase
And still the waters with thine eyes!

The Crag-fast sheep

Unhappy heedless sheep! 'tis all in vain!
These walls of rock thou never canst ascend;
Thou canst not leap the cliff nor climb again
That slippery path by which thou late didst wend.

The winds of night will beat upon thy head,
No shelter hast thou from the raging storm:
Ravens will on thy mouldering corse be fed,
And crowd to tear thy hunger-wasted form.

'Bindweed whiter e'en than lilies'

Bindweed whiter e'en than lilies
Who has given you all your snow?
'Twas the lovely Amaryllis
She our whiteness did bestow:
She bequeathed to us in dying
All her hand's surpassing snow;
See her cheeks beside us lying
On the eglantine they glow.

'The hart delights in cooling streams'

The hart delights in cooling streams
When noonday suns are blazing high:
In tribulation's scorching beams
The heart of man is cheered by streams
That flow from Pity's tearful eye.

The birth of purple Columbine

Bright Flora found young Cupid weeping
With tears a lifeless turtle steeping:
'Unkind Mischance!' cries he, 'to waft
'Gainst that fair breast my ill-sped shaft'.
The Goddess vows, to soothe his pain
That, if he'll dry those tears again,
Where sweet Columba closed her eyes
A plant of somber hue shall rise,
Whose petals deftly interlaced,
And on a slender pillar placed,
The dove's fair form shall represent,
A still fresh-springing monument.

Forget me not

''Mid all the clang of battle field
Thy voice, Melane, I shall hear,
'Mid flashing helm and burnished shield
Those radiant eyes my heart will cheer'.

'Ah! gentle Maid forget not me,
And wear this ring of tourquois blue'.
How joys the Knight her tears to see!
With bounding heart he bids adieu.

The Knight is gone to the far Crusade,
Of glittering troops a captain bold:
The lady seeks the lonely glade,
Where strays the rivulet clear and cold.

The Knight beholds the azure deeps
And hills with sunny palms overgrown;
Melane by the cypress weeps
And gazes on her tourquois stone.

A Lordling seeks that Maiden's love,
But she her faith will ne'er resign,
He pulls in sport her silken glove,
'Let this at least', he cries, 'be mine'.

And with the glove the ring he drew:
And now 'tis in the limpid stream:
Like tearful eyes of tenderest blue
Those gems amid the waters gleam.

'An omen that my love shall speed!
Sink, hapless ring', exclaimed the Youth:
'Nay thus', cried she, 'the omen read,
That I shall ne'er forget my truth'.

'O let oblivion drown the spell,
That keeps Melane's soul from me!' –
'What Time has perfected so well
By Time shall ne'er dissolved be'.

That ring the lady ne'er regains;
'Tis lost beneath the weedy floor;
Her hand the tempter ne'er obtains
On velvet mead or willowy shore.

Glad Spring returns, with zephyr bland,
To scatter buds and bells around:
The Knight comes home from Paynim land,
And Love is now with roses crowned.

The lovers seek the murmuring nook:
Of weary combats each can tell:
They stand beside the favourite brook,
Beneath whose wave the keepsake fell.

Behold a flow'r of purest blue
Bestows its beauty on the spot:
The Warrior blest his Lady true,
And called its name *Forget me not.*

The Staining of the Rose

The Queen of Beauty weeps amain
To hear her harmless Dove complain
That yonder Rose, so fondly prest,
Has wounded her confiding breast;
That bosom which in love she sought,
With all inviting odours fraught,
As soft and snowy as her own,
Such cruel treachery has shown,
Betrayed her to the ambushed thorn,
Her bosom pierced, her vesture torn!
Then thus the Queen of Flow'rs upbraids
The culprit Rose: 'Go seek the shades! –
Henceforth that tell-tale crimson stain,
Ne'er to be cleansed by dew or rain,
Shall fix a blush upon the breast,
Where Love in safety could not rest'.

'No joy have I in passing themes,'

No joy have I in passing themes,
I cannot smile my friends to cheer:
Then be it mine to cherish dreams,
And hide, if not repress, the tear.

No more I do a mother's part;
My life's sad scene a weary bed;
Then silent be my breaking heart,
I'll be as still as I were dead.

'When Herbert's Mama was a slim little Maid'

When Herbert's Mama was a slim little Maid
And lived among Waterfalls, Mountains and Lakes,
With Edith her cousin she rambled and played,
And both of them gardened with spades and with rakes.

Sweet Edith was fair as the lilies and peach,
And swift as the slender Gazelle's were her feet.
And over her forehead the small silken curls
Waved yellow and light as the clusters of Wheat.

A Wood full of harebells was close to their home
It led to a River all broken with rocks:
They loved o'er the thyme and the heather to roam
'Mid branches and brambles they ruined their frocks

They tucked up their trowsers to paddle and wade
And washed their Doll's clothes in the Waters so cold
They wove pretty garlands within the cool shade
Their May-Pole was beauteous indeed to behold.

In winter they put on their great wooden Clogs
And down to the Lake with young Derwent they ran
The Sun having chased all the vapours and fogs
Their sport on the Ice in high glee they began.

In Summer they gathered the primroses pale
And filled little Baskets with fruits and with flowers,
To make Primrose Wine, and their friends to regale
Was one of their pleasures in Summer's gay hours.

With Dora and Mary they went to the Grove
And picked purple bilberries near the bright Lake:
They oft with each other in gathering strove
An excellent pie did their bilberries make.

They frequently sat on the bough of a Tree
And climbed to the top of a very high beech
They sought for the foxgloves and O with what glee
They gathered the globe flowers that grew within reach!

Summer

And art thou here again, thou beamy Summer,
And are thy trees again with garlands hung?
Gay birds are welcoming the bright newcomer
As once I welcomed thee when life was young.

No more for me those rainbow garlands wave
I cannot smile to see thee pranked so fine;
'Twere all as well with flow'rs to dress my grave
As weave thy wreath for eyes bedimmed like mine.

I know that joy even in youth's joyous day
Is fresh at morn, by eve a flowret wan;
I know that even in the year's decay
Live hues as fair as those for ever gone.

Ah well I wot for many a heart thy beams
Can but illumine Memory's scene of woe:
That many a Maniac's agonizing dream
Blazes more fiercely in thy ardent glow.

I ask not health nor yet the youthful heart
To view this glowing world in crystal shrined:
I ask but strength to play my passive part
Pow'r to resign those joys with steadfast mind.

Come Patience to my couch with all thy wealth:
No longer then I'll struggle to be free;
For thee I pray without thee what were Health?
Ah why desert who prays for only thee?

The lamb in the Slough

Shepherd Shepherd haste away!
This is not a time to play;
Let not buxom Amaryllis
Hold you by a chain of lilies:
For the youngest of your flock
Underneath a frowning rock
In the mire is sticking fast,
There 'tis like to breathe its last,
While the Raven round it flies
Ready to peck out its eyes.

The Water Lily

A lovely damsel in a lake was drowned
Her garments green were floating on the wave,
A golden brooch her snowy head-dress crowned,
In gay attire she found a watery grave.

On that most fatal spot a lily grew
And spread on either side her verdurous leaves;
The blossom white with stud of golden hue
Still gently heaving as the water heaves.

Like this fair flow'r from earth the maiden came
Now blooms perennial in bright Heaven's eye;
A grosser element matured her frame
This world of tears prepared her for the sky.

The Pair that will not meet

My youthful compeer once was rosy Health
She led me forth beside the sparkling rills;
But Love by Fortune ruled came but by stealth,
And while my feet were bounding o'er the hills
This heart was heavy with a load of care;
Mine eyes turned inward on a shadowed mind:
That Lake was bright – but Henry was not there:
In vain does Nature smile when Love's unkind.

Youth shed around me his ethereal light;
Seen through those beams this face awhile seemed fair;
If not of heavenly mould 'twas soft and bright,
As Earth illumined may with Heaven compare:
But then I cried O flowers of fleeting bloom
Thy lavish blossoms lead to wan decay;
O couldst thou wither now and life resume
In Henry's sight to flourish fresh and gay!

Now Love is mine – his bounteous feast hath spread –
'Come taste' he cries 'I give thee Angel's food:
Such balmy fruits of such a glowing red
The touch of innocence in Eden wood'.
Alas while Love this richest banquet brought
Youth stole away and Health with eye askance
Froze every glad desire and genial thought
And left me gazing in a joyless trance.

With heart unblest I feed on viands rare
And tears are mingled with nectarous draught:
Return sweet Health and bless my dainty fare
What gales of happiness thy pinions waft!
But if thy coming sends Love's face away
And if ye two can never end your strife
Then Love though joyless I with thee must stay
To part now from thee were to part from Life.

Written on a blank leaf of 'Naturalist's' Magazine

My Derwent! may you study Nature's book
O'er hill and dale, by Lake and winding brook
And may it lead your steps to many a glade
And coy recess, in choicest charms arrayed
Though none but bashful birds inhabit there
And Insects shy – and blossoms bright and rare
But should that God who guided Nature's hand
Take what he gave – thy youthful powers demand,
Should weary Couch and watchful nights make part
Of that probation which must mould the heart
For realms where strength 'with gentleness keeps pace'
And Beauty shrinks not from Time's sterner race,
Still may you dwell on Nature's brilliant page
And while such books as these your eyes engage
Thought their faint portraiture shall far outgo
And make earth's brightest hues before you glow.

*Sara Coleridge to her dear Nephew Derwent Moultrie Coleridge
composed this hot rainy Morning July 19 1834*

May Derwent be studious learned and wise,
And delight in the things of earth, water and skies.

Young Days of Edith and Sara

When Godmama Edith and Herbert's mama
Were living together near Keswick's bright Lake
They clomb up great Skiddaw with Edith's papa
And oft did a journey in Borodale take.

In Summer they sat on the bough of a tree
And often they climbed to the top of the beech:
They went to the river the globe flow'rs to see
And often transplanted the roots they could reach.

In Winter they put on their great wooden clogs
And down to the Lake with their comrades they ran;
The Sun having chased all the vapours and fogs
Their sport on the ice in high glee they began.

In Summer they loved by the river to play
And was their doll's frocks in the water so cold;
In heaping up stones they spent many a day
But ne'er did an end to their labours behold.

As soon as the bridge was about three parts done
A great heavy rainfall was sure to ensue:
The river would then with great violence run:
Away went the bridge – not a stone left in view.

The Plunge

When good Uncle Derwent was quite a young boy
To fish in the Lake was his frequent employ:
His sister one day was indulged in her wish
To carry his basket when he went to fish.

'Twas pleasant to see the line bob in and out,
With Brandlin and Perch almost equal to trout:
Blue Dragonflies over the water were skimming,
And silvery minnows within it were swimming.

And now with the pebbles she played duck and drake,
Now looked at the Heron that flew o'er the lake:
She found purple bilberries juicy and good,
And columbines tall in a neighbouring wood.

At last 'mid the waves little Sara espies
Some fine water-lilies with bright yellow eyes:
And, thoughtlessly eager to make them her own,
She skipped from the shore to a glistening stone.

From it she expected the lilies to reach:
But this very stone had been brought from the beach
By fisherman Derwent who on it had set
His great naked feet which with wading were wet.

So while his poor sister was pulling a lily,
Not thinking how soon she'd be made to look silly,
While o'er the broad leaves and white blossoms she bent,
Down, down with a plunge in the water she went.

The place was quite shallow, she soon scrambled out;
Her brother, astonished, set up a loud shout:
Her home was far distant, and more than a mile
She ran hardly stopping except at a stile.

A gentleman met her in grievous distress,
And, staring amazed at her dripping white dress,
He held up his hands cast his eyes to the sky,
And said neither 'how do you do', nor 'good bye'.

The narrow Escape

Young Sylvia was an active child,
She clomb the tree like squirrel wild,
And skipping in her frock of green
The fern and foxglove-bells between,
While feathery birches round her trembled
A grass-hopper she much resembled.
Her chirping blithe, her merry tune
Was like the insect's voice at noon.
One day with Dora she was roaming
Where Rydal's mountain beck was foaming;
To hear the rooks in Rydal-grove,
And trace that changeful brook they rove,
That brook which now an emerald seems,
Now shows the sapphire's azure gleams,
Betwixt its glistening rocky setting
Which blue and lilac buds are fretting.
'By yonder cliff my way I'll take!'
Cried Sylvia. 'Then your neck you'll break!'
So said the mirthful dimpling Dora,
With looks as gay and fresh as Flora:
With blossoms crowned with blossoms laden
Like Flora looked the bonny maiden.
But Sylvia's on a slender ledge

And gathering bluebells o'er its edge:
Now to proceed is her intent,
And so to aid the hard ascent
She seizes on a jutting stone
Which giving way she's roughly thrown
Close to the deep and bubbling well
Below the Force of Rydal Fell.
The waterfall is roaring loud:
The spray is like a glittering cloud;
But now there sounds a noisier din
The fallen damsel's brain within
And mists before her eyes are swimming
Than spray more thick and sight-bedimming.
Sweet Dora who had stood aghast
While all this wild adventure past
Now trembled like that trembling spray,
Or reeds on which the breezes play:
And white was gentle Dora's cheek
Which lately showed so bright a streak,
Fair likeness of the dashing stream,
Fair contrast to the rosy gleam
Of those bright wreaths of eglantine
Which now her power-less hands resign.
But Dora's cheek regains its bloom:
This is not Sylvia's day of doom:
And dimples 'mid her roses play
When Sylvia laughs her fears away.
'Dora!' she cried, 'cast off your trance;
You see I've scaped my two-fold chance;
I'm neither drenched in Rydal-pool,
Nor lamed too much to play the fool'.
So on they wandered by the rill
Their hands and laps with flow'rets fill:
And Dora's love was somewhat wiser
Than that of many an old adviser:
Her joy she showed at Sylvia's 'scape,
Nor said 'I warned you of the scrape';
She thought a bruise and sudden shock
Would keep her from the dangerous rock
And make the giddiest pate more wary
Without a wordy commentary.

'See the Halcyon fishing'

See the Halcyon fishing
O'er the glassy stream
All the air's transparent,
What a sunny gleam!
This is lovely weather,
'Tis a Halcyon day,
Sure a storm's impending
Let us haste away.

Daffodil or King's Spear

A fairy knight went forth to fight,
He a golden helmet wore,
And the spear he shook with might
All in vert was painted o'er.
The battle's done and in the lake
He his burning thirst must slake;
While he quaffs the silver tide
All his armour lays aside.

Now the fairy tribes advance:
Gladsome is their acclamation;
He has freed them with his lance
He must rule the grateful nation;
He as king must rule the realm;
Ne'er resume his magic helm,
Wear instead a jewelled crown,
Sceptre wield and spear lay down.

Memory of that joyous day
Thus hath Flora fair decreed,
Never more must pass away
Those bright arms are fruitful seed.
Thence the daffodil hath sprung
All with yellow helmet's hung;
Thence her verdant leaf doth rear
Image of a fairy spear.

Fine birds and their plain wives

The Peacock is magnificent – he wears a splendid crest,
He's like an Indian Rajah in his richest regal vest;
With robes of purple velvet and a jewel gleaming train
He struts before his wifie who is simple neat and plain.

The Turkey dresses handsomely he makes a proud display,
Like puffy rustling dowager in all her court array;
What topazes and tourquoises the foreign Turkey wears!
His mistress plain and motherly for splendour little cares.

The gaudy bird of China with his waving plumes of gold
And bright vermilion bodice is as fine as he is bold:
The Pheasant wears a snowy ring and flaming scarlet patch:
His wifie in her quaker dress can scarcely be his match.

And Chanticleer's a kingly bird with noble arching tail:
His dunghill is a throne of state which none will dare assail:
He wears a crimson cravat and a fiery coloured comb;
The Hen's a homely housewife and her dress is fit for home.

The cocks of every family are given to the duel;
They all are gallant combatants – in battle fierce and cruel:
Their beaks are sharp and potent – they have spurs upon their legs:
The hens have no such weapons – they are made for laying eggs.

The Glow-worm

Glow-worm lights her starry lamp
'Mid the mosses soft and damp
Softer radiance I'll avouch
Streams not on a Princely couch;
Wherefore in the murky night
Shines the Glow-worm's chrysolite.
Dian's crescent diadem
Scarce can show a lovelier gem.
Thus she thinks her spouse to guide
Thus she lures him to her side,
She's his jewel bright and pure

She's his earthly cynosure:
She's his fair and brilliant bride,
Helpmate given his way to guide.
Thus to wed an earthly dame
From the skies young Cupid came;
Spouses if you all had wings
Who would trust to wedding rings?

The Glow-worm

'Mid the silent murky dell
Glow-worm glitters on the rock,
But they say her Curfew bell
Ever sounds at twelve o'clock.
When the ghosts at midnight vanish
She her tender star must banish;

Ere the nightingale is mute,
Ere the stars begin to fade
Ere the lover stops his lute,
Stops his tuneful serenade
Nature's living chrysolite
Shines no more amid the night!

When bindweed shuts her azure cup
And eyes as blue are sealed in sleep
And fairies by the [?moonlight] sup
And flowers the sun's departure weep
Then doth the Glow-worm's tender light
Gleam amid the murky night.

And yet they say her Curfew bell
Doth ever sound at twelve o'clock
Ere the pipe of Philomel
Yields to the clarion of the cock
Ere the lover stops his lute
Ere his pleading voice is mute.

When tearful eyes asleep are laid
When gloaming ghosts of midnight vanish
When stars on high begin to fade
The Glow-worm waves dim and wannish
Then is quenched the [?lowliern] star
Nature's living breathing spar.

Herbert looking at the Moon

While my little prattling treasure
Looks upon the spangled skies,
I with more than equal pleasure
View his sparkling starry eyes:
Those young eyes so blue and bright
Bless me with their joyous light.

Hark my darling shouts aloud,
Luna's playing hide and seek:
Now she goes behind the cloud,
Now she shows her radiance meek,
Thus his face so round and beaming,
Gladdens me with changeful gleaming.

P'rhaps some day with lengthened face
Musing on his earthly Hebe
Now no more a [?proto-space]
He may gaze on thee, bright Phœbe!
Vowing that his brilliant maid
Throws thy splendours into shade.

Thus like many another youth
All intent on love and marriage
He will go beyond the truth
And his earlier love disparage:
May his loved one wear a mien
If not brilliant still serene!

Some day p'rhaps a hoary sage,
Wearing out each youthful hope,
Seeking light to cheer his age,
Peering through his telescope,
He on Luna's face may gaze,
Soothing thus his latter days.

Game

On Scotland's stormy hilltops the Ptarmigans alight,
And when the snow's their carpet their plumes are snowy white;
But when the snow is melted and hills are growing green
In greenish speckled garments the Ptarmigans are seen.

On Scotland's purple moorlands in Autumn's pleasant weather
Upsprings the whirring moorcock from out the fern and heather
His haunts are reddish russet and his feathers ruddy brown
But soon the Kite will seize him, or sportsman bring him down.

In woody dell or marsh land the darkest grouse are bred
In Devon's hilly region where frowning rocks are spread
About the dusky shingle and plashy banks of peat
They spread their sable pinions or glide with feathered feet.

Amid the bristling stubble or turnips' tender green
Dame Partridge with her speckled brood may frequently be seen:
In colour like the brown clods or buffish withered stalks
They flit before the farmer while o'er the field he walks.

How oft amid the brushwood in yellow tinted copse
The Pheasant's ruddy plumage is stained with ruddy drops;
Amid the golden harvest in safety he may steal
But when the sickle reaps it the bullet he must feel.

'From Isles far over the sea'

From Isles far over the sea
   Where lofty Palms are growing
I built my nest in a blossoming tree
   While spicy gales were blowing.

I laboured hard my house to build
With ravening mouths it soon was filled;
Alas I've plenty of leisure now
I've nought to do on the greenwood bough.

An ape in a piebald vest
A most accomplished vaulter
Leapt on to the bough which held my nest
I wished the knave a halter.

The monkey children shake my cage
And pluck my tail to rouse my rage:
But those with tails and hairy brows
I see no more on the greenwood boughs.

Seek first the Kingdom of Heaven

We speak of pansies in rich velvet drest,
Of daffodil and woodbine 'well attired';
Or say smooth lilies wear a silken vest,
That so their beauty may be more admired;
Yet finer are the textures, thus exprest,
Than vain luxurious monarch e'er desired;
Nor costliest web twice dipped in Tyrian dye,
With peony's deep blush did ever truly vie.

Ev'n as the rainbow, in mid heav'n suspended,
Paints to a thinking heart th' Almighty mind,
His mercy, pow'r, and love divinely blended, –
So these fair colours, wondrously combined,
These earthly rainbows o'er the plains extended.
Footsteps of One whom they who seek shall find,
May faintly picture to man's musing sight
The glories kept in store for all that love the light.

Calmly they show their splendour to the sun
In rich apparel with no labour sought,
Emblems of blessed Saints that heav'n have won,
Who, *clothed upon*, beyond our human thought,
In robes for which they neither toiled nor spun,
Bright robes by Jesus earthly travail bought,
Shed fragrant incense 'mid celestial air,
And still more fragrant dews with all around them share.

If God so richly gems each hidden glade
With flow'rs profuse – a seeming reckless waste, –
And scatters radiance o'er the forest shade
In tangled wilds by human foot untraced,
While secret caves, in lucid spars arrayed,
Might seem as if for courtly pageant graced,
What splendours shall his own Elect surround
When they in open Heav'n with Christ Himself are crowned!

Will God then clothe me too in garments fine,
Which stateliest monarch's richest robe exceed,
Whilst I like lilies that in sunlight shine
Look up to Heav'n, nor for myself take heed?
Nay! Thou in haste must seek the realm divine,
There to receive some far more glorious weed;
How he shall clothe thee doth not yet appear:
Christ as He is none see while yet they sojourn here.

To frame a nest where he shall never dwell
The silk-worm spins, for others' profits caring;
The ocean insect forms a coral cell,
Then leaves the glosey home for others' wearing;
And fish, that slowly shape the wreathed shell,
Spend all the day in each day's need preparing;
A house not made with hands our toils may gain,
Where we may dwell for aye exempt from toil and pain.

Our toils a prize which human skill and force
Could ne'er have fashioned surely may obtain.
Christ's are the amaranth flowers that crown the course,
But we must run that deathless wreath to gain:
As waters flowing from a lofty source
In some high-seated reservoir remain,
His merits are already stored on high,
''Tis ours to climb the steep and to that flood draw nigh'.

A Sister's Love

When o'er my dark and wayward soul
The clouds of nameless Sorrow roll;
When Hope no more her wreath will twine
And Memory sits at Sorrow's shrine;
Nor aught to joy my soul can move
I muse upon a Sister's Love.

When tired with study's graver toil
I pant for sweet Affection's smile,
And rich with restless hopes of fame,
Would half forgo the panting aim
I drop the book, – and thought will rove,
To greet a Sister's priceless Love.

When all the world seems cold and stern,
And bids the bosom vainly yearn;
When Woman's heart is lightly changed,
And Friendship weeps o'er looks estranged;
I turn from all the pangs I prove
To hail a Sister's changeless Love.

And, oh, at shadowy close of even,
When Quiet rings the soul to Heaven;
When the long toils of lingering day,
And all its cares, are swept away;
Then – while my thoughts are rapt above –
Then more I prize my Sister's Love.

From Petrarch

O! 'tis blessed to muse o'er the past hours of Youth,
When the Soul's purest visions start up like the truth;
While Memory brings back the images bright
And fancy enshrines them in colours of light!
Then untainted by grief and uninjured by years,
Like an Angel of Heaven the loved one appears.
Then the ringlets of gold and the bosom of snow
Then the sun on the cheek just beginning to blow,
Then the magic of joy in her eye's glance of blue,
Then the swell of the heart and the love for aye true,
And the last word she spoke and the last farewell sigh
Shed a blessing around, tho' for ever gone by.
   I see the loved spot on the brink of a river
That dances and foams and runs sparkling for ever
When the last time I met thee thy soft form I claspt
Fair Spirit! What years since what ages have past!
In that lovely bower with myrtles o'erhung
Where the jasmin and roses their rich fragrance flung
I saw thee half sitting half lying, sweet Maid!
With a bloom in each cheek that made the sun fade.
'Twas wondrous to watch as the soft gale passed there
How the flow'rs fell in wind-woven wreaths on her hair
And eager to kiss her bright bosom descended
Like jasmin and roses and blue violets blended
While she meekly bent 'neath the amorous showers
Looked glorious and lovely this Queen of the flowers.
Some fell like a fringe on the garment she wore
Some fell on the face and some fell on the shore
Some dancing around and around in the air
Seemed dancing to say 'Balmy Love's reigning here'.
I [?sighed] as I gazed in a fair dream of bliss
If Heaven's but a Paradise what then is this?
Hark! Hark! The dream's gone but the sound's in my ears
And pure as she was once again she appears
Farewell 'tis the last time – our loves the fates sever
Shall I e'er again hear her? – Oh! never! Oh! never.

Poems from Phantasmion

Note: The 35 poems are presented in the order in which they appear in the book. I have added brief prefatory remarks to give an indication of the context in the story.

Chapter 2. The fairy Potentilla has given the young Prince Phantasmion wings and the power of flight. 'This choral strain resounded' from a chorus of insects in 'the groves and flowery meads below'.

See the bright stranger!
On wings of enchantment,
See how he soars!
Eagles! that high on the crest of the mountain,
Beyond where the cataracts gush from their fountain,
Look out o'er the sea and her glistering shores,
Cast your sun-gazing eyes on his pinions of light!
Behold how he glitters
Transcendantly bright!

Whither, ah whither,
To what lofty region
His course will he bend?
See him! O, see him! the clouds overtaking,
As tho' the green earth he were blithely forsaking;
Ah now, in swift circles behold him descend!
Now again like a meteor he shoots through the sky,
Or a star glancing upward,
To sparkle on high!

Chapter 5. Princess Iarine, overheard by Phantasmion, sings a plaintive song about her mother Anthemmina, presumed to be dead.

Tho' I be young – ah well-a-day!
I cannot love these opening flowers;
For they have each a kindly spray
To shelter them from suns and showers;
But I may pine, oppressed with grief,
Robbed of my dear protecting leaf.

Since thou art gone, my mother sweet,
I weep to see the fledgling doves
Close nestling in a happy seat,
Each beside the breast it loves;
While I, uncared for, sink to rest,
Far, far from my fond mother's breast.

Sweet mother! in thy blessed sight
I too might blossom full and free;
Heaven then would beam with softer light;
But, could I rest upon thy knee
My drooping head, what need I care
How sickly pale and wan I were?

My face I view in pools and brooks,
When garish suns full brightly shine;
Ah! me! think I, those blooming looks,
And that smooth brow can ne'er be mine!
Sad heart! I charge thee to express
More truly all thy deep distress.

Deceitful roses leave my cheek,
Soft lilies join those happy flowers,
Which nothing stirs but zephyr meek,
Which nought oppresses but sweet showers;
While she lies dead I grieve to be
More like those living flowers than she.

O, what to me are landscapes green,
With groves and vineyards sprinkled o'er,
And gardens where gay plants are seen
To form a daily changing floor?
I dream of waters and of waves,
The tide which thy sea-dwelling laves.

Dearly I love the hours of night,
When bashful stars have leave to shine;
For all my visions rise in light,
While sun-lit spectacles decline;
And with those starts they fade away,
Or look as glow-worms look by day.

Chapter 8. Overheard by Phantasmion, the Princess Leucoia (sister of Karadan and Zelneth) sings to a white stag 'who seemed to be conscious that he was the subject of the strain'.

Sylvan stag, securely play,
'Tis the sportful month of May,
Till her music dies away
 Fear no huntsman's hollo;
While the cowslip nods her head,
While the fragrant blooms are shed
O'er the turf which thou dost tread,
 None thy traces follow.

In the odours wafted round,
Those that breathe from thee are drowned;
Echo voices not a sound,
 Fleet one, to dismay thee;
On the budding beeches browse,
None shall come the deer to rouse;
Scattered leaves and broken boughs
 Shall not now betray thee.

Sylvan deer! on branches fed,
'Mid the countless branches bred,
Mimic branches on thy head
 With the rest are springing;
Smooth them on the russet bark,
Or the stem of cypress dark,
From whose top the woodland lark
 Soars to heaven singing.

Bound along or else be still,
Sportive roebuck, at thy will;
Wilding rose and woodbine fill
   All the grove with sweetness
Safely may thy gentle roe
O'er the piny hillocks go,
Ever-white robed torrent's flow
   Rivalling in fleetness.

Peaceful breaks for thee the dawn.
While thou lead'st thy skipping fawn,
Gentle hind, across the lawn
   In the forest spreading:
Morn appears in sober vest,
Nor hath eve in roses drest,
By her purple hues exprest,
   Aught of thy blood-shedding.

Chapter 8. The song is continued by the voice of Zelneth, Leucoia's sister, 'which proceeded from the dell, and which was joined by one of deeper tone, in these latter verses'. The other voice is that of Karadan, her brother and Phantasmion's rival for Iarine.

Milk-white doe, 'tis but the breeze
Rustling in the alder trees;
Slumber thou while honey-bees
   Lull thee with their humming;
Though the ringdove's plaintive moan
Seem to tell of pleasure flown,
On thy couch with blossoms sown,
   Fear no peril coming.

Thou amid the lilies laid,
Seem'st in lily vest arrayed,
Fanned by gales which they have made
    Sweet with their perfuming;
Primrose tufts impearled with dew;
Bells which heav'n has steeped in blue
Lend the breeze their odours too,
    All around thee blooming.

None shall come to scare thy dreams,
Save perchance the playful gleams;
Wake to quaff the cooling streams
    Of the sunlit river;
Thou across the faithless tide
Needest not for safety glide,
Nor thy panting bosom hide
    Where the grasses shiver.

When the joyous months are past,
Roses pine in autumn's blast,
When the violets breathe their last,
    All that's sweet is flying:
Then the sylvan deer must fly,
'Mid the scattered blossoms lie,
Fall with falling leaves and die
    When the flow'rs are dying.

Chapter 8. Phantasmion overhears Karadan singing a love song.

One face alone, one face alone,
    These eyes require;
But, when that longed-for sight is shewn,
    What fatal fire
Shoots through my veins a keen and liquid flame,
That melts each fibre of my wasting frame!

One voice alone, one voice alone,
    I pine to hear;
But, when its meek mellifluous tone
    Usurps mine ear,
Those slavish chains about my soul are wound,
Which ne'er, till death itself, can be unbound.

One gentle hand, one gentle hand,
    I fain would hold;
But, when it seems at my command,
    My own grows cold;
Then low to earth I bend in sickly swoon,
Like lilies drooping 'mid the blaze of noon.

Chapter 10. Arzene, the mother of two boys and two girls, denies that she favours
her elder son over the other children.

Deem not that our eldest heir
Wins too much of love and care;
What a parent's heart can spare,
    Who can measure truly?
Early crops were never found
To exhaust that fertile ground,
Still with riches 'twill abound,
    Ever springing newly.

See in yonder plot of flowers
How the tallest lily towers,
Catching beams and kindly showers,
    Which the heav'ns are shedding:
While the younger plants below
Less of suns and breezes know,
Till beyond the shade they grow,
    High and richly spreading.

She that latest leaves the nest,
Little fledgling much carest,
Is not therefore loved the best,
    Though the most protected;
Nor the gadding daring child,
Oft reproved for antics wild,
Of our tenderness beguiled,
    Or in thought neglected.

'Gainst the islet's rocky shore
Waves are beating evermore,
Yet with blooms 'tis scattered o'er,
   Decked in softest lustre:
Nature favours it no less
Than the guarded still recess,
Where the birds for shelter press,
   And the hare-bells cluster.

Chapter 11. Zelneth is disappointed because she suspects that Phantasmion does not love her but Iarine.

While the storm her bosom scourges,
What can calm a troubled sea?
Will the heaving dashing surges
Tranquil through persuasion be?
Rest, my soul, like frozen ocean!
Let thy wavy tumult sleep!
Rise no more in vexed commotion,
Heedless where the gale may sweep.

Clouds that have the light partaken,
Round yon radiant planet rolled,
Lingering in the west forsaken,
Soon shall glimmer, wan and cold:
All our thoughts are gay and golden,
While the sun of hope they shroud;
Those bright beams no more beholden,
Turn again to watery cloud.

He that scorns the smiling valley,
Fragrant copse and gentle stream,
Forth for distant heights to sally,
Whence deceptive colours gleam;
Late shall find that cold and dreary,
'Tis but from afar they glow,
Shall not, when his feet are weary,
Win the blossomed vale below.

Chapter 11. Phantasmion's song is a sort of reply to Zelneth's.

Many a fountain cool and shady
May the traveller's eye invite;
One among them all, sweet lady,
Seems to flow for his delight:
In many a tree the wilding bee
Might safely hide her honeyed store;
One hive alone the bee will own,
She may not trust her sweets to more.

Say'st thou, 'Can that maid be fairer?
'Shows her lip a livelier dye?
'Hath she treasures richer, rarer?
'Can she better love than I?'
What formed the spell, I ne'er could tell,
But subtle must its workings be,
Since, from the hour, I felt its pow'r,
No fairer face I wish to see.

Light winged Zephyr, ere he settles
On the loveliest flower that blows,
Never stays to count thy petals,
Dear, delicious, fragrant rose! –
Her features bright elude my sight,
I know not how her tresses lie;
In fancy's maze my spirit plays,
When she with all her charms is nigh.

Chapter 12. Hearing a thrush's song in the woods, Leucoia 'softly warbled these words'.

The captive bird with ardour sings,
Where no fond mate rewards the strain,
Yet, sure, to chant some solace brings,
    Although he chant in vain:
But I my thoughts in bondage keep,
Lest he should hear who ne'er will heed,
And none shall see the tears I weep,
    With whom 'twere vain to plead.

No glossy breast, no quivering plume,
Like fan unfurled to tempt the eye,
Reminds the prisoner of his doom,
    Apart, yet all too nigh:
O would that in some shrouded place
I too were prisoned fancy free,
And ne'er had seen that beaming face,
    Which ne'er will beam on me!

When kindred birds fleet o'er the wave,
From yellow woods to green ones fly,
The captive hears the wild winds rave
    Beneath a wint'ry sky!
And, when my loved one hence shall fleet,
Bleak, bleak will yonder heav'n appear,
The flowers will droop, no longer sweet,
    And every leaf be sere.

Chapter 13. The old and infirm King Penselimer, still grieving about his desertion years before by his lover Anthemmina, sings from 'that gloomy cell, in which it is his pleasure to immure himself'.

The sun may speed or loiter on his way,
May veil his face in clouds or brightly glow;
Too fast he moved to bring one fatal day,
I ask not now if he be swift or slow.

I have a region, bathed in joyous beams,
Where he hath never gilded fruit or flower,
Hath ne'er lit up the glad perennial streams,
Nor tinged the foliage of an Autumn bower.

Then hail the twilight cave, the silent dell,
That boast no beams, no music of their own;
Bright pictures of the past around me dwell,
Where nothing whispers that the past is flown.

Chapter 13. Penselimer sings another song. 'Alas!', says one of his listeners, 'his are but mockeries of woe, that dwell in the wild brain and never touch the heart'.

Grief's heavy hand hath swayed the lute;
    'Tis henceforth mute:
Though pleasure woo, the strings no more respond
    To touches light as fond,
Silenced as if by an enchanter's wand.

Do thou brace up each slackened chord,
    Love, gentle lord;
Then shall the lute pour grateful melodies
    On every breeze,
Strains that celestial choristers may please.

Chapter 14. 'A tinkling melody rang out from the rocks overhead. It seemed as if they were musical stones touched by some invisible hand with a silver hammer, and soon they seemed to speak thus', with cryptic prophecies about Iarine (Anthemmina's daughter) and Phantasmion (king of Palmland).

Life and light, Anthemna bright,
Ere thy knell these rocks shall ring,
Joy and power, a gladdening dower,
Thou shalt shower on Palmland's king.
Floor of coral, roof of beryl,
Thou shalt find afar from peril,
While thy lovely child is dwelling
Where the palm and vine are swelling,
Crystal streams around her welling,
All the land her virtue telling.
Life and light, Anthemna bright,
Thou to Palmland's king art bringing:
Richest dower, fairest flower
Is from thee for Palmland springing.

Chapter 16. The wicked Queen Maudra sings a lullaby to her infant child,
thinking that he is soon to be killed by the water-witch Seshelma.

O sleep, my babe, hear not the rippling wave,
Nor feel the breeze that round thee lingering strays,
    To drink thy balmy breath,
    And sigh one long farewell.

Soon shall it mourn above thy wat'ry bed,
And whisper to me, on the wave-beat shore,
    Deep murm'ring in reproach,
    Thy sad untimely fate.

Ere those dear eyes had opened on the light,
In vain to plead, thy coming life was sold,
    O! wakened but to sleep,
    Whence it can wake no more!

A thousand and a thousand silken leaves
The tufted beech unfolds in early spring,
    All clad in tenderest green,
    All of the self same shape:

A thousand infant faces, soft and sweet,
Each year sends forth, yet every mother views
    Her last not least beloved
    Like its dear self alone.

No musing mind hath ever yet foreshaped
The face tomorrow's sun shall first reveal,
    No heart hath e'er conceived
    What love that face will bring.

O sleep, my babe, nor heed how mourns the gale
To part with thy soft locks and fragrant breath,
    As when it deeply sighs
    O'er autumn's latest bloom.

Chapter 17. The child Albinet has been frightened, and entreats his half-sister Iarine 'to soothe him for a while with one of her soft melodies': 'she sang words like these'.

How gladsome is a child, and how perfect is his mirth,
How brilliant to his eye are the daylight shows of earth!
But Oh! how black and strange are the shadows in his sight,
What phantoms hover round him in the darkness of the night!

Away, ye gloomy visions, I charge ye hence away,
Nor scare the simple heart that without ye were so gay;
Alas! when you are gone with all your ghastly crew,
What sights of glowing splendour will fade away with you!

He'll see the gloomy sky, and know 'tis here decreed,
That sunshine follow every storm, and light to shade succeed,
No more he'll dread the tempest, nor tremble in the dark,
Nor soar on wings of fancy far beyond the soaring lark.

I love thee, little brother, when smiles are on thy face,
I love thy eager merriment, thy never failing grace:
But when the shadow darkens thee and chills thy timid breast,
I'd watch from eve till daybreak that thou might'st be at rest.

Chapter 18. Karadan is plotting to win Iarine's love by magic means, but fears he will never do so. Alone 'on a turfy bank', overseen only by Phantasmion, he 'softly murmured these words'.

I tremble when with look benign
Thou tak'st my offered hand in thine,
Lest passion-breathing words of mine
    The charm should break:
And friendly smiles be forced to fly,
Like soft reflections of the sky,
Which, when rude gales are sweeping by,
    Desert the lake.

Of late I saw thee in a dream,
The day-star poured his hottest beam,
And thou, a cool refreshing stream,
    Didst brightly run:
The trees where thou wert pleased to flow,
Swelled out their flowers, a glorious show,
While I, too distant doomed to grow,
    Pined in the sun.

By no life-giving moisture fed,
A wasted tree, I bowed my head,
My sallow leaves and blossoms shed
    On earth's green breast:
And silent prayed the slumbering wind,
The lake, thy tarrying place, might find,
And waft my leaves, with breathings kind,
    There, there, to rest.

*Chapter 19. The disguised Phantasmion joins in a drinking chorus with the pages
and servants of the royal household of King Albinian and Queen Maudra.*

Ne'er ask where knaves are mining,
While the nectar plants are twining:
    To pull up the vine
    They never incline,
With all their deep designing.

O ne'er for the dead sit weeping,
Their graves the dews are steeping:
    And founts of mirth
    Spring up from the earth,
Where they are at peace and sleeping.

Away with studious learning,
When heaven's bright lamps are burning:
    In the glorious art
    That gladdens the heart,
We cannot be more discerning.

Forget the blood that gushes
Where the fiery war-horse rushes:
   The blood that glows,
   As it brightly flows,
Is making us chant like thrushes.

When burdened troops, advancing,
In cumbrous mail are glancing,
   With garlands crowned
   We reel around,
While the earth and sky are dancing.

*Chapter 20. Phantasmion 'heard the inmates of the chamber', Iarine and her little
    brother Albinet, 'greeting the dawn with this song'.*

How high yon lark is heavenward borne!
Yet, ere again she hails the morn,
Beyond where birds can wing their way
Our souls may soar to endless day,
May hear the heavenly quires rejoice,
While earth still echoes to her voice.

A waveless flood, supremely bright,
Has drowned the myriad isles of light;
But ere, that ocean ebbed away,
The shadowy gulf their forms betray,
Above the stars our course may run,
'Mid beams unborrowed from the sun.

In this day's light what flowers will bloom,
What insects quit the self-made womb!
But ere the bud its leaves unfold,
The gorgeous fly his plumes of gold,
On fairer wings we too may glide,
Where youth and joy no ills betide.

Then come, while yet we linger here,
Fit thoughts for that celestial sphere,
A heart which, under keenest light,
May bear the gaze of spirits bright,
Who all things know, and nought endure
That is not holy, just, and pure.

Chapter 20. Iarine fears that the disguised Phantasmion is an enemy and magician, and sings 'over and over again, in concert with Albinet, a few verses which her mother had taught her'. Between the stanzas Phantasmion pleads his love and good will, interrupting the song at 'Gentle spirit –'.

Newts and blindworms do no wrong,
Spotted snakes from guilt are clear;
Smiles and sighs, a dang'rous throng,
Gentle spirit, these I fear;
Guard me from those looks of light,
Which only shine to blast the sight.

Serpents' tongues have ne'er been known
Simple maid from peace to sever,
But the voice whose thrilling tone
Tells of love that lasts for ever,
Gentle spirit –

Beetles black will never charm me,
Spiders weave no snares for me,
Thorny hedge-hogs cannot harm me,
But the brow where heaven I see,
Catching beams from sunny eyes, –
Guard me from that bright disguise!

Chapter 20. Iarine joins her father Albinian in a song about the blight of infidelity in love.

The winds were whispering, the waters glistering,
A bay-tree shaded a sun-lit stream;
Blasts came blighting, the bay-tree smiting,
When leaf and flower, like a morning dream,
    Vanished full suddenly.

The winds yet whisper, the waters glister,
And softly below the bay-tree glide;
Vain is their cherishing, for, slowly perishing,
It doth but cumber the river side,
    Leafless in summer-time.

Chapter 22. Phantasmion's enemy, Glandreth, wants to win Iarine even though he is much older than she. He has dropped 'a painted roll' which is 'all embla-zoned with gay devices, in the midst of which Phantasmion read these lines'.

False Love, too long thou hast delayed,
Too late I make my choice;
Yet win for me that precious maid,
And bid my heart rejoice,
Then shall mine eyes shoot youthful fire,
My cheek with triumph glow,
And other maids that glance desire,
Which I on one bestow.

Make her with smile divinely bland
Beam sunshine o'er my face,
And Time shall touch with gentlest hand
What she hath deigned to grace;
O'er scanty locks full wreaths I'll wear;
No wrinkled brow to shade,
For joy will smooth the furrows there,
Which earlier griefs have made.

Though sports of youth be tedious toil,
When youth has passed away,
I'll cast aside the martial spoil
With her light locks to play;
Yea turn, sweet maid, from tented field
To rove where dewdrops shine,
Nor care what hand the sceptre wield,
So thou wilt grant me thine.

Chapter 26. Iarine has been captured by Ulander, who wants her for his bride. Overheard 'with grieved heart' by Ulander, she sings about Phantasmion, whom she is beginning to love.

He came unlooked for, undesired,
A sun-rise in the northern sky:
More than the brightest dawn admired,
To shine and then for ever fly.

His love, conferred without a claim,
Perchance was like the fitful blaze,
Which lives to light a steadier flame,
And, while that strengthens, fast decays.

Glad fawn along the forest springing,
Gay birds that breeze-like stir the leaves,
Why hither haste, no message bringing,
To solace one that deeply grieves?

Thou star that dost the skies adorn,
So brightly heralding the day,
Bring one more welcome than the morn,
Or still in night's dark prison stay.

Chapter 27. Phantasmion goes in search of Iarine, 'and this was one of many strains with which he addressed her'.

Yon changeful cloud will soon thy aspect wear
So bright it grows: – and now, by light winds shaken,
O ever seen yet ne'er to be o'ertaken!
Those waving branches seem thy billowy hair.
The cypress glades recall thy pensive air;
Slow rills, that wind like snakes amid the grass,
Thine eye's mild sparkle fling me as they pass,
Yet murmuring cry, This fruitless quest forbear!
Nay e'en amid the cataract's loud storm,
Where foamy torrents from the crags are leaping,
Methinks I catch swift glimpses of thy form,
Thy robe's light folds in airy tumult sweeping;
Then silent are the falls: 'mid colours warm
Gleams the bright maze beneath their splendour sleeping.

Chapter 28. Zelneth, in love with Phantasmion, has drugged him with a love potion. 'Already she fancied herself the flower-crowned bride of Phantasmion, and breathed in a soft lulling melody this happy strain.'

I was a brook in straitest channel pent,
Forcing 'mid rocks and stones my toilsome way,
A scanty brook in wandering well nigh spent;
But now with thee, rich stream, conjoined I stray,
Through golden meads the river sweeps along,
Murmuring its deep full joy in gentlest undersong.

I crept through desert moor and gloomy glade,
My waters ever vexed, yet sad and slow,
My waters ever steeped in baleful shade:
But, whilst with thee, rich stream, conjoined I flow,
E'en in swift course the river seems to rest,
Blue sky, bright bloom, and verdure imaged on its breast.

And, whilst with thee I roam through regions bright,
Beneath kind love's serene and gladsome sky,
A thousand happy things that seek the light,
Till now in darkest shadow forced to lie,
Up through the illumined waters nimbly run,
To show their forms and hues in the all revealing sun.

Chapter 30. Zelneth, now separated from Phantasmion, 'continued her weeping, or murmured laments like these'.

By the storm invaded
Ere thy arch was wrought,
Rainbow, thou hast faded
Like a gladsome thought,
And ne'er mayst shine aloft in all earth's colours fraught.

Insect tranced for ever
In thy pendent bed,
Which the breezes sever
From its fragile thread,
Thou ne'er shalt burst thy shell and crumpled pinions spread.

Lily born and nourished
'Mid the waters cold,
Where thy green leaves flourished,
On the sunburnt mould
How canst thou rear thy stem and sallow buds unfold?

Snowy cloud suspended
O'er the orb of light,
With its radiance blended
Ne'er to glisten bright,
It sinks, and thou grow'st black beneath the wings of night.

*Chapter 31. Ulander, son of the witch Malderyl, has at different points of the
story wooed both Zelneth and Iarine. 'After his departure Phantasmion read these
lines which he found traced on a tablet, but whether addressed to Zelneth or Iarine
seemed uncertain.'*

I thought by tears thy soul to move,
Since smiles had proved in vain;
But I from thee nor smiles of love,
Nor tears of pity gain:
Now, now I could not smile perforce
A sceptred queen to please:
Yet tears will take th'accustomed course
Till time their fountain freeze.

My life is dedicate to thee,
My service wholly thine:
But what fair fruit can grace the tree
Till suns vouchsafe to shine?
Thou art my sun, thy looks are light,
O cast me not in shade!
Beam forth ere summer takes its flight,
And all my honours fade.

When, torn by sudden gusty flaw,
The fragile harp lies mute,
Its tenderest tones the wind can draw
From many another lute;
But when this beating heart lies still,
Each chord relaxed in death,
What other shall so deeply thrill,
So tremble at thy breath?

Chapter 33. Sailing in 'a mother-of-pearl boat, which was drawn by a team of swans', the captive enchantress Melledine 'began to murmur a soft melody', aiming to delude the listening Leucoia into pursuing her unreturned passion for Phantasmion. 'The tone of her voice was inexpressibly sweet.'

Blest is the tarn which towering cliffs o'ershade,
Which, cradled deep within the mountain's breast,
Nor voices loud, nor dashing oars invade:
Yet e'en the tarn enjoys no perfect rest,
For oft the angry skies her peace molest,
With them she frowns, gives back the lightning's glare,
Then rages wildly in the troubled air.

This calmer lake, which potent spells protect,
Lies dimly slumbering through the fires of day,
And when yon skies, with chaste resplendence decked,
Shine forth in all their stateliest array,
O then she wakes to glitter bright as they,
And view the face of heaven's benignant queen
Still looking down on hers with smile serene!

What cruel cares the maiden's heart assail,
Who loves, but fears no deep felt love to gain,
Or, having gained it, fears that love will fail!
My power can soothe to rest her wakeful pain,
Till none but calm delicious dreams remain,
And, while sweet tears her easy pillow steep,
She yields that dream of bliss to ever welcome sleep.

Chapter 34. The fairy Potentilla rebukes Melledine and consoles Leucoia.

What means that darkly-working brow,
              Melledina?
Whose heart-springs art thou wresting now,
              Melladina?
The dearest pleasure follows pain,
But thou with grief shalt aye remain,
And for thyself hast forged the chain,
              Melladina!

Ah, dream of sullen skies no more,
               Sad Leucoia!
The roughest ocean hath a shore,
               Sweet Leucoia!
A steadfast shore the billows kiss,
And often some fancied joy to miss,
Prepares the heart for higher bliss,
               Young Leucoia!

Chapter 35. Mischievously urged on by Malderyl, Melledine 'began to sing thus in the person of Ulander' to the listening Phantasmion, Ulander, Leucoia and Zelneth.

Methought I wandered dimly on,
But few faint stars above me shone,
    When Love drew near:
'The night,' said he, 'is dark and damp,
To guide thy steps receive this lamp
    Of crystal clear'.

Love lent his torch, − with ready hand
The splendid lamp by his command
    I strove to light;
But strove in vain; no flame arose,
Unchanged, unfired as moonlit snows,
    It sparkled bright.

Again on wings as swift as thought
The boy a glittering cresset brought
    Of sunny gold:
Full sure 'twas worth a monarch's gaze,
And how I toiled to make it blaze
    Can scarce be told.

Deprived of hope I stood perplexed,
And, through my tears, what offered next
    Obscurely floated:
One other lamp Love bade me take,
Mine eye its colour, size or make,
    But little noted;

Till soon, (what joys my soul inspire!)
From far within a steady fire
   Soft upward steals;
And O how many a tender hue,
What lines to loveliest nature true,
   That beam reveals!

Now what reck I of burnished gold,
Or crystal cast in statelier mould? –
   This lamp be mine,
Which make my path where'er I go,
With warm reflective colours glow,
   And light divine.

*Chapter 39. Arzene is wandering in search of her son Karadan. 'With tearful eyes
Arzene murmured this song, and seemed to see the childish form of Karadan
sporting before her, as when she sang it first.'*

'The spring returns, and balmy budding flow'rs
Revive in memory all my childish hours,
When pleasures were as bright and fresh, though brief,
As petals of the May or silken leaf.

But now when kingcups ope their golden eyes,
I see my darling's brighten with surprise,
And rival tints that little cheek illume
When eglantine displays her richest bloom.

Dear boy! thou art thy mother's vernal flow'r,
Sweeter than those she loved in childhood's hour,
And spring renews my earliest ecstasy,
By bringing buds and fresh delights for thee.'

Chapter 39. Arzene hears a shepherdess singing 'while her flocks nibbled the green grass' on the margin of a brook. 'These were the words of her song.'

Full oft before some gorgeous fane
The youngling heifer bleeds and dies;
Her life-blood issuing forth amain,
While wreaths of incense climb the skies.

The mother wanders all around,
Through shadowy grove and lightsome glade;
Her foot-marks on the yielding ground
Will prove what anxious quest she made.

The stall where late her darling lay
She visits oft with eager look:
In restless movements wastes the day,
And fills with cries each neighbouring nook.

She roams along the willowy copse,
Where purest waters softly gleam:
But ne'er a leaf or blade she crops,
Nor couches by the gliding stream.

No youthful kine, though fresh and fair,
Her vainly searching eyes engage;
No pleasant fields relieve her care,
No murmuring streams her grief assuage.

Chapter 39. Arzene's quest for Karadan is nearly over: waiting to join him, she 'continued to watch the restless ocean, oft reverting in thought to this strain, which had been sung in happier days amid the blooming bowers of Polyanthida'.

See yon blithe child that dances in our sight!
Can gloomy shadows fall from one so bright?
    Fond mother, whence these fears?
While buoyantly he rushes o'er the lawn,
Dream not of clouds to stain his manhood's dawn,
    Nor dim that sight with tears.

No cloud he spies in brightly glowing hours,
But feels as if the newly vested flowers
  For him could never fade;
Too well we know that vernal pleasures fleet,
But having him, so gladsome, fair, and sweet,
  Our loss is overpaid.

Amid the balmiest flowers that earth can give
Some bitter drops distil, and all that live
  A mingled portion share;
But, while he learns these truths which we lament,
Such fortitude as ours will sure be sent,
  Such solace to his care.

*Chapter 42. Phantasmion and his allies join battle with Glandreth in the valley of
the Black Lake. Seen at a distance, the enemy is 'hailed by the men of Palmland
with this chant'.*

Their armour is flashing,
And ringing and clashing,
Their looks are wild and savage!
With deeds of night
They have darkened the light,
They are come from reckless ravage!
O bountiful earth,
With famine and dearth,
With plague and fire surround them;
Thy womb they have torn
With impious scorn;
Let its tremblings now confound them!
Our cause maintain,
For as dew to the plain,
Or wind to the slumbering sea,
Or sunny sheen
To woodlands green,
So dear have we been to thee.

The new-blown flowers,
From thy fairest bowers,
Their rifling hands have taken;
And the tree's last crop,
That was ready to drop,

From the boughs have rudely shaken;
Through deep green dells,
Where the bright stream wells,
Like diamond with emerald blending;
Through sheltered vales,
Where the light wind sails,
High cedars scarcely bending;
Through lawn and grove,
Where the wild deer rove,
They have rushed like a burning flood:
For morning's beam,
Or the starry gleam,
Came fire, and sword, and blood.

Then lend us thy might,
Great Earth, for the fight,
O help us to quell their pride:
Make our sinews and bones
As firm as the stones,
And metals that gird thy side;
May the smould'ring mountains,
And fiery fountains
Inflame our vengeful ire,
And beast that lurk
In thy forests' murk,
Their tameless rage inspire;
While from caves of death
Let a sluggish breath
O'er the spoilers' spirits creep;
O send to their veins
The chill that reigns
In thy channels dark and deep.

But if those we abhor
Must triumph in war,
Let us sink to thy inmost centre,
Where the trump's loud sound,
Nor the tramp and the bound,
Nor the conqueror's shout can enter;
Let mountainous rocks,
By earthquake shocks,
High o'er our bones be lifted;
And piles of snow,

Where we sleep below,
To the plains above be drifted;
If the murderous band
Must dwell in the land,
And the fields we love to cherish,
From the land of balm
Let cedar and palm
With those that reared them perish.

Chapter 43. A farewell dirge sung by sea-nymphs for Anthemmina, the mother of Iarine. The two were reunited before Anthemmina died on the barren peninsula to which she had been exiled.

Ah, where lie now those locks that lately streamed
'Mid gales that fanned in vain the fevered cheek?
    Low let them rest, ye winds,
    The heart now rests in peace.

How vainly, while the tortured bosom heaved,
Restless as waves that lashed the sea-beat haunt,
    We strove to cool that cheek
    Which death too quickly chilled!

Like wreaths of mist that some lone rock o'erhang,
And seem intent to melt the crags away,
    While with soft veil they hide
    Its tempest-riven head;

We hovered round thee on the lonesome beach,
And sought to calm thy brow with dewy hand,
    Thy wild unquiet eye
    With pitying glances met.

'O fly with us,' we whispered; 'from glad hearts,
From mirthful bands that meet on moon-light shores,
    We came to watch thee pace
    This melancholy strand.

'A captive thou, an exile here confined;
But fatal passion to more galling chains,
    To exile more unblest,
    Thy blinded spirit dooms.

'O fly with us; no dangerous choice we know,
Mild heavenly influence guides our gentle lives,
　　Obedient as yon tide,
　　Swayed by the circling moon.

'O fly with us, free, free as ocean gale,
To roam at large, released from sorrow's power.' –
　　Ah no! – far happier scenes,
　　More blissful change, be thine!

Through fields of radiance let thy spirit stray,
While these fair relics, shrined in ocean's depth,
　　Shall gleam like purest pearl,
　　Caressed by winds and waves.

Chapter 44. 'The face of the deep, with its changeful hues and emotions, for the mind of Iarine, was her mother's monument, and strains like these she dedicated to her memory.'

Poor is the portrait that one look portrays,
It mocks the face on which we loved to gaze;
A thousand past expressions all combined,
The mind itself depictured by the mind,
That face contains which in the heart is shrined.
Yet, dearest mother, if on lasting brass
Thy very self to future times might pass,
Ill could I bear such monument to build
For future times with dearer memories filled:
Ah no! thy fadeless portrait in my breast
From earth shall vanish when I sink to rest;
But, ere to join thee on glad wings I go,
Thy sun-like influence, beaming here below,
In sorrow's hour, when earthly hope betrays me,
To heav'n above, my hope's best aim, shall raise me,
In hours of bliss when heav'n almost seems here,
For thy sweet memory claim the tribute tear;
So yon bright orb doth tearful incense gain
From glittering lake, swift rill, and humid plain,
Yet dries the spray that trembled in the shower,
And shines reflected from each dripping flower.

The Three Humpbacked Brothers

Three queer little brothers lived once at Bagdad;
Their tempers were sorry, their persons were bad;
For each on his back had a notable hump;
And each of them looked like a pollarded stump.

These Humpies were cutlers and clever ones too:
Through steel they obtained gold and silver anew;
For many a stout swordsman or noble would stop
To purchase the armour that brightened their shop.

One morning, as two of this beautiful three
Were wending together a neighbour to see,
They met, by ill fortune, a nobleman's son,
A youth much addicted to frolic and fun.

'Fair creatures', cried he, 'with what joy should I jump,
If one of you would but lend me his hump!'
'Take that!' cried the foremost, and gave him a poke:
To jeer at a cutler he found was no joke.

The wounded man's Father was vastly concerned;
Against both the brothers he blustered and burned:
To hold them he soon made the city too hot;
And so they made off to a far-away spot.

While *they* roamed about in regret and vexation,
The butt of ill luck and a prey to starvation,
Their brother at home was increasing his store,
And hoping they'd never come back any more.

Not seeing his person reflected in theirs,
He fancied it handsome and gave himself airs,
And thought it no very bad change in his life
To part with two brothers and take to a wife.

The wand'rers at last, having heard of his wealth,
Resolved they would creep to his mansion by stealth;
Both felt a desire, which they scarce could repress,
To render his over-grown wealth somewhat less.

'He'll hearken', said they, 'to our pitful moan,
He's flesh of our flesh, and he's bone of our bone;
He's fashioned, 'tis plain, on the very same block:
And surely he'll open his door when we knock'.

By night they stole forth to his house at Bagdad,
And there an unbrotherly greeting they had;
'Hence wretches!' he cried, with a voice loud as thunder
'Your weapons of blood cut our union asunder'.

A brother devoid of affections fraternal
Is much like a nut that has never a kernel;
The wife, who had taken the brute for his money,
Compared to her husband, was sweeter than honey.

To her, in his absence, one day they applied;
They coaxed and entreated, and blubbered and sighed;
And she, being told that her charms were divine,
Would charm them still more with her bread, meat and wine.

But now the snug party are caught in a trap;
They hear an imperative ratta-tap-tap;
'There! stow yourselves down, 'mid the casks in the vault!'
The housewife exclaims, and they run without halt.

While they in the cellar squat down in the dark,
The dame at the door is admitting her spark,
Who snapped, snuffed and snarled like an ill-natured hound;
But ne'er smelt the rats which were lodged underground.

Again he goes forth to his spouse's delight;
She hies to the cellar and sees a strange sight:
For there lie the Humpies apparently dead,
And each near a hogshead reclining his head.

I've heard about rats, that grew tipsily frisky
By dipping their tails into bottles of whisky:
Invention is sharpened good liquor to win,
But senses steal out as the nectar flows in.

No mourning had they from their sister-in-law;
She carefully shrowded them under some straw;
And then with posthaste a stout Porter she fetches,
And shows number one of the two little wretches.

Says she, my good fellow, just lend me your back;
And shut up your mouth, though you open your sack:
Convey to the river what there you behold,
And when you return you shall carry off gold.

The Porter obeyed without hint or remark;
The way to the Tigris he knew in the dark;
He heard, he was certain, a pop and a splash,
And fully expected to handle the cash.

But when he got back, just conceive his affright! –
He seems to behold by the Camp's gloomy light
The very same man with a hump on his back,
Whom lately he carried away in a sack!

The lady exclaimed, 'How you stare like a dunce!
Why don't you go off with the body at once?'
This Porter's broad back, if the truth must be said,
Was harder and stronger by far than his head.

'I own Ma'am', said he, 'I'd have readily sworn,
That this here odd fellow these shoulders had borne,
That down to the brink of the river he went,
And into the depth of the current was sent:

'But since there he lies, all my words to confute,
This business I'll do without further dispute'.
So thinking his heretofore journey a dream,
The second poor tippler he lodged in the stream.

Again he returns and draws nigh to the door,
And looks all around him, behind and before;
He lifts up his hand and is going to knock;
And now lets it fall and stands still as a stock.

And why does his vigour thus suddenly fail?
Has he spied a ghost by the moonlight pale?
He thinks he espies, and his flesh doth quiver,
The very same man he has flung in the river.

For sturdily strutting, as who but he,
Home comes the third of the hump-backed three:
How little he thinks, as he draws to the door,
That he never shall enter that house any more!

Whatever we secretly do that is wrong
Will rise to waylay and torment us ere long;
So thought the stout Porter, whose conscience was sold;
And yet he determined to pocket the gold.

'For shame!' bellowed he, 'is it thus ye conspire
To cheat a poor hard-working man of his hire?
This time I'll take care you shall play me no tricks,
The next ground you tread is the border of Styx'.

Next moment he's hoisting him over his back,
Along with a stone tightly tied in his sack;
He bears to the river this ponderous lump,
And overboard shoves it and down it goes plump.

Then back he repairs to the house of the dame,
Advance of his wages intending to claim:
And tells her the trouble and plague he has had,
And whom he had met in the streets of Bagdad:

And how, without waiting to dawdle and talk,
He stopped him at once in the midst of his walk;
And how he would never more walk upon earth;
And how much hard cash such a service was worth.

The widow has heard his long tale to an end;
And now she begins her long tresses to rend;
And now she begins to lament and to rave,
And calls the stout Porter a blundering slave.

'You've murdered my husband! – 'tis really too bad! –
The sweetest and handsomest man in Bagdad;
This guerdon from me you may certainly hope,
A stout bastinado and lastly a rope'.

The Porter perceived that she said what she meant,
By steps which she took to fulfil her intent;
This truth in his mem'ry she chose to refresh,
That no one should come 'twixt the nail and the flesh,

And now she is publicly making her wail,
And telling the justice a pitiful tale;
When two of the Hunchbacks astonish her sight,
Both much better able to tell it aright.

For they had swum out of their terrible scrape;
And, not being bagged, had the power to escape;
On touching the water revived from their swoon,
And struggled to land by the light of the Moon.

Their brother his life was unable to save;
He did not lie under the sod but the wave;
But though he had ne'er shed a tear in his life,
Those waters were swelled by the tears of his wife.

A suitor at length this young widow consoled,
Well-made and good-natured and not without gold;
His brothers came in for two thirds of the money,
And married fair maids though their persons were funny.

By presents they managed their foes to appease,
And softened the hearts of the wrathful grandees;
To cutlery each of them gave up his mind,
But cutting and maiming for ever declined.

'Tis wrong to give thrusts or hard thumps in a passion,
To drink in a cellar's a very bad fashion;
But hard'ning the heart and denying the purse
To poor starving brothers I reckon much worse.

Reflections on Reading Lucretius

A child beholds the clear blue skies
And thinks that azure tract is Heav'n –
A happy land, where nothing dies
No cows and sheep to slaughter driv'n,
And where those birds and lambkins go
Whose death he oft has mourned below.

The golden lakes with violet shores
Beside them how he longs to play –
To stir the sleeping flood with oars
And toss about like new-mown hay
Those cloudlets white as drifted snow
Which melt not in the sunny glow.

Up there amid the starry crowd
No hour of night he'd give to sleep
But hide behind a gilded cloud
And then start forth with sudden leap
To meet bright Luna face to face
Or find her in her hiding place.

The grave he fears is dark and cold,
How long do people tarry there?
How can they heave up all the mould
And come again into the air
To seek that winding path sublime
By which to Heav'n above they climb.

But when he hears the thunder groan
And sees the rapid lightning fly,
He speaks of Heav'n with altered tone
He could not bear to dwell on high
Where flames might rush into his face
And loud commotions shake the place.

Ev'n so our ancestors untaught
Placed in that Heav'n immortal Pow'rs
Seeing it so divinely wrought
While clouds, mists, lightning, rainbows, showers
Sun moon and stars remotely ranging
Told them of Gods bright and unchanging.

The threatening murmurs of the sky
Black shades and silence of the night
The vehement voices heard on high
When adverse winds rush forth to fight
And Heav'n with dreadful torches fired
A trembling worship once inspired.

Can turbulence and bitter strife
(So spake the old poetic sage)
Flow from the Lords of Light and Life?
O wretched men! what war ye wage
With your own peace who thus can deem
Making sad earnest of a dream.

Is he the pious man that bends
All humbly veiled before a stone?
Victims to every altar sends
And prostrate near proud temples thrown
Spreads out his palms in abject fear
Tow'rd stocks which neither see nor hear?

The Sun is glorious in his might,
Lakes, rivers, earth's unnumbered streams,
And ocean multiply his light –
Mean are *our* sacrificial steams,
And unglad offerings do we give
To him by whom in joy we live.

A virgin Goddess pure and mild
Of the soft moon might fancy frame
But men with sorceries have defiled
Thy beauteous image and thy name –
And thou the kindest loveliest best
Must minister to deeds unblest.

Where wert thou gliding p'rhaps unshrowded
With even a momentary veil
When Trivia's Aulic fane was crowded
With Grecian chiefs awe-stricken and pale
Who dream that favouring gales will rise
If murdered one soft virgin dies?

Clad like thyself in modest splendour
Sweet Iphianassa seeks the coast,
Nor finds at need one [?true] defender
In all that heav'n revering host:
The lovelier she – the more divine
The worthier gift for Dian's shrine.

Called from her home to marriage bands
She enters that unhallowed fane –
No bridegroom by the altar stands –
Vain are her hopes, her tremblings vain
Whom Hymen's torch, all over-bright,
Shall ne'er distress with garish light.

She sees her Father's tearless grief
While tears break forth from all around –
Her locks like Autumn's affluent sheaf
With no mere festal fillet bound –
The sword concealed with piteous care
His eyes but not her breast to spare.

Speechless she kneels nor strives in vain
Martyred without a martyr's crown –
Poor Maid! – thy Sire will cross the main
Borne by strong winds to high Renown. –
But thee no kingly Sire avails
Thou ne'er shalt view his streaming sails.

Such bad religion flows from fear –
He truly owns a pious mind
Who scans unmoved th'empyreal sphere
Nor asks what architect designed
Those temples – nor by what control
The luminous orbs their courses roll.

When Thunder traverses Heav'n's vault
He sinks not on a suppliant knee
Fear strick'n lest some unpunished fault
Has roused a [?ling'ring] deity –
Nor when high tow'r and Forest nod
Hears in the wind a blustering god.

Oft driven along the billowy regions
By vehement winds careering fast
With all their elephants and legions
Great generals tremble at the blast
And pray for softly-heaving seas
With sails full swoll'n by one kind fav'ring breeze.

In vain! – the wind unheeding raves
They sink – by sudden whirl overthrown
Engulphed between uprushing waves –
As if some Sovereign force unknown
All human things – all pow'r and state
Loved to deride and desecrate
And crush with overwhelming weight.

He with true piety is blest
Who holds at nought the lurid gleams
Of [?Tartarus?] by [——] spirits possest
Nor dreads the labyrinthine streams,
(Spectres of which bring stifled sleep)
Which round that shadowy region creep –

Vain boast! this imagery of gloom
Rivers that loud lamenting roll
Their waves which sunbeams ne'er illume
Such visions tranquillize the soul
Which misery pain and toils unblest
Prefers to everlasting rest.

The feelings of our earliest years
Th'imaginings of ardent youth
Unreasoning wonder – hopes and fears
Contain dim shadows of the truth
And taught by Heav'n we still avow
That men can see but shadows now.

from 'Kings of England from the Conquest'

Richard II, surnamed of Bordeaux. 1377

One thousand three hundred and twenty seven
Came Richard the Second to sov'reign power;
By Hereford he from power was driven,
Was forced to submit at Milford Haven,
And perished a prisoner in the Tower.
   Wicliffe now began to preach
   His tenets met with condemnation:
   Yet many a wholesome truth they teach,
   And led the way to the Reformation.

Henry IV, of Bolingbroke. 1399

One thousand three hundred and ninety nine
Henry the fourth usurped the throne;
Against him Scots and Welsh combine
Rebellions cause him many a groan:
    Dan Chaucer now began to write;
    A statesman and a poet he;
    He oft is called and with good right,
    The Father of English poetry.

Henry V, of Monmouth. 1413

The year one thousand four hundred thirteen
Did Harry the fifth to power advance;
The Frenchmen hear his name with spleen,
Because of his triumphs in boastful France.
    As Prince of Wales he lived but ill;
    As King he gained a good report:
    Ten thousand Frenchmen his soldiers kill
    In gaining the battle of Agincourt.

★ ★ ★ ★

Henry VIII. 1509

The year one thousand five hundred and nine
Brought Henry the eighth to rule the nation;
A despot strong and a weak divine
He lent a hand to the reformation.
That hand he did encarnadine
With blood of some in lofty station:
Most of his wives, as I opine,
Had cause to rue their elevation.

Edward VI. 1547

One thousand five hundred and forty seven
Edward the sixth to the throne was raised:
He went in early youth to Heaven
For piety, zeal and learning praised.

Mary I, or Queen Mary Tudor (vulgarly 'bloody Queen Mary').

One thousand five hundred and fifty three
Began Queen Mary's fiery reign;
The worst of counselors had she,
And an evil spouse in Philip of Spain.

The meek usurper fair Jane Grey,
By others placed in Mary's way,
Just after Edward's dying day,
Did with her life the forfeit pay,
When came the Queen to sovereign sway.

James I. 1602

It happed in one thousand six hundred and two
That James the First to kingship rose
A Prince to reformed religion true:
But Raleigh's death his weakness shows.

Charles I, called 'King Charles the Martyr'.

One thousand six hundred and twenty five
Began the reign of 'Charles the Martyr':
In his time parties strongly strive:
Each thinks its cause the country's charter;
In course of time the desperate strife
Cost the monarch his crown and life.

Oliver Cromwell, the Protector. 1649

One thousand six hundred and forty nine
Cromwell rose to be England's head:
'They who against the Lion combine
Suffer a Wolf', say some, 'in his stead'.
Others account him a hero fine:
Though discontent around him spread:
His ends were good, as they opine,
Whate'er of his sterner deeds be said.

Charles II. 1660

In sixteen hundred and sixty we find
The crown restored to Charles the Second;
A Prince to pleasure much inclined,
Who witty more than wise was reckoned.

James II. 1685

One thousand six hundred and eighty five
James the Second took kingly state:
He chose for his Popish faith to strive
And so was obliged to abdicate,
In the famed Revolution of eighty eight.

William and Mary. 1689

One thousand six hundred and eighty nine
William and Mary both were crowned.
The virtues of Mary brightly shine
And William's vict'ries were renowned.

★ ★ ★ ★

George III. 1760

One thousand seven hundred and sixty A.D.
George the Third, his grandson reigned;
A true born Englishman was he
And stoutly England's cause maintained.
Th'Americas long his mind distressed;
They for their freedom boldly stirred;
While England foreign foes suppressed
Reason forsook poor George the Third.

George Prince Regent. 1810

It happed in one thousand eight hundred and ten
His son as Regent began to reign;
Great was the pride of Englishmen
When Wellington triumphed on Waterloo's plain.

George IV. 1830

It happed in thousand eight hundred and twenty
That George the Fourth was King enthroned:
Peace we had but strife in plenty
When the King his Queen disowned.
The Cato Street plot affrighted the nation
Ere a month of his reign was past;
The Romanists gained emancipation
The year before he breathed his last.

William IV. 1830

In eighteen hundred and thirty the realm
William the Fourth to rule was sent;
Then Earl Grey was at the helm, –
Gave us reform of Parliament.

Queen Victoria. 1837

In eighteen hundred and thirty seven
Fair Victoria became our Queen:
May her reign by the grace of heaven
Still be prosp'rous and serene.

Finis.

Receipt for a Cake

Take Flour made from Wheat most fine
Take Currants fresh from Zante's Isle, –
Take Butter from the choicest Kine
Take Almonds from the Trees that smile

On Jordan's banks: – take of the Spice
That in the Indian Isles abound;
Take new-laid Eggs, quite fresh and nice,
Take Sweetmeats, richest that are found;

Take of the Wine that Falstaff loved –
Take eau de vie from Gallia's shore,
Take of the Sugar most approved
That's grown upon Jamaica's shore,

And when you've beat and mixed them well,
And let them in your Oven bake:
Rest them awhile, before you tell
The glories of the splendid Cake.

Then cover it with snowy hue
Of Eggs and Sugar finely spread,
And Waters richly perfumd through
The Orange Flower's fragrant aid

Then set it on a festive board
All gaily decked with Flowers so fair,
Bid Flora all her sweets afford
And scatter choicest Roses there.

And let the Myrtle there be found
Its blooming flower – its lasting leaf
And Violets shed their perfume round,
And Cornflower with the golden sheaf

And next arrange a choice repast,
And blithely fill the sparkling Bowl;
While round the board may gather fast
A group whose joy knows no control.

And chiefest – dearest – loveliest there
Will march a prized and blooming Bride
And watch the manliest form, most fair
Sit raptured by the Maiden's side.

While favoured friends both old and young
Are come this Pair so blest to meet,
Favours are given and Bells are rung,
And cheerful healths their Union greet.

Then cut the Cake and send it round,
Where other friends more distant dwell
Packets with snow-white ribbon bound,
The welcome vows shall quickly tell.

Then Youths and Maidens love to try
Their future fate in mystic dream,
And to the bridal Ring apply,
And trust the Cake will kindly seem

And let their guileless Fancy roam
On *one* whose love may long endure
And twine around some future home
Their radiant wreath of joy most pure.

Lines on the Death of ——

The dappled pink and blushing rose
    In bloom with one another vie
And what the brightness they disclose
    To Laura's cheek of vermeil dye
The azure cope of yonder sky
    That bends so brightly over all
Whate'er in Nature meets the eye
    Seems but one vast funereal pall.

In every flower I trace decay
    A worm I see in softest bloom
For Henry bloomed as bright as they
    Now dark with shadows of the tomb
And see but death in many a face
    That ne'er has felt the touch of time.

The dappled pink and blushing rose
    In brightness with each other vie
And Laura's lips and cheeks disclose
    A richer softer livelier dye
The sapphire of yon vaulted sky
    That bends so brightly over all
Whate'er of beauty meets my eye
    Seems but one vast funereal pall.

For my Father on his lines called 'Work Without Hope'

Father, no amaranths e'er shall wreathe my brow, –
Enough that round thy grave they flourish now: –
But Love 'mid my young locks his roses braided,
And what cared I for flow'rs of deeper bloom?
Those too seemed deathless – here they never faded,
But, drenched and shattered, dropped into the tomb.

Ne'er was it mine t' unlock rich founts of song,
As thine it was, ere Time had done thee wrong: –
But ah! how blest I wandered nigh the stream,
Whilst Love, fond guardian, hovered o'er me still!
His downy pinions shed the tender gleam
That shone from river wide or scantiest rill.

Now, whether Winter 'slumbering, dreams of Spring',
Or, heard far off, his resonant footsteps fling
O'er Autumn's sunburnt cheek a paler hue,
While droops her heavy garland here and there,
Nought can for me those golden gleams renew,
The roses of my shattered wreath repair,
Yet Hope still lives, and oft, to objects fair
In prospect pointing, bids me still pursue
My humble tasks: – I list – but backward turn
Objects for ever lost still struggling to discern.

'Friend, thou hast been a traveller bold;'

Friend, thou hast been a traveller bold;
   Thine eyes, men say, have served thee well!
Now say if thou didst e'er behold
   The wondrous sight that I shall tell.

A tree in perfect beauty growing –
   To whose wide branches clusters cleave
Of fruit as rich and golden glowing
   As that which tempted mother Eve.

A glorious plant of perfect beauty,
   Its branches hung with clustered flowers,
Rich fruit like that which led from duty
   Frail Eve mid Eden's happy bowers.

And grafted in that noble stock
   Full many a cankered, crooked shoot,
As if the foster stem to mock,
   Laden with harsh and bitter fruit.

Sight such as this no eye can see
   For every graft partakes the juices,
Like saplings of its foster tree
   And fruitage of like kind produces.

And grafted in this noble stem
   Full many a cankered, withered shoot,
Which men would to the flames [?condemn]
   Because they bear such worthless fruit.

To a fair young Lady who declared that she and I were coevals

Art thou then one of my compeers?
   Can this surprising tale be truth?
Dost thou sustain the weight of years
   That crushed in me the soul of youth?

With how light steps must Time have gone,
   My softly-blooming friend, o'er thee! –
What shoes of lead has he put on
   To leave these livid marks on me!

For thy dear sake did he forego
   The rude unwelcome ways he hath?
Would that he always journeyed so –
   Thus rather brushed than trod his path!

And Nature – by what kind caprice
   Hath she forborne those lustrous locks –
Preserved for thee a young lamb's fleece
   Amid the dusky full-grown flocks?

But perhaps I read your meaning wrong
   And this you'd have me take for true,
That I, who seem to have lived so long
   Am yet no older, Sweet, than you.

Well! 'tis a bright creative thought,
   A rich and most enriching blindness;
Youth's roses, long so vainly sought,
   Spring up beneath that gaze of kindness.

I'll keep the fairy gifts you bring
   With all the rest that Time has granted;
No shade advancing years can fling
   On charms by Love and Fancy planted.

To a Fair Friend arguing in support of the theory of the renovation in a literal sense of the material system

Philonous to Hylasia

1

Keep, oh keep those eyes on me,
     If thou wouldst my soul persuade,
Soul of reasoner bold and free,
     Who, with pinions undismayed
Soars to realms of higher worth
Than aught like these poor heavens and earth.

2

Talk no more of Scripture text,
     Tract and note of deep divine:
These but leave the mind perplexed –
     More effectual means are thine:
Through that face, so fair and dear,
The doctrine shines as noon-day clear.

3

Who that sees the radiant smile
     Dawn upon thy features bright,
And thy soft, full eyes the while
     Spreading beams of tender light,
But must long those looks to greet,
Where perfect souls in joyance meet?

4

Who that round some verdant home
     Day by day with thee hath strayed,
Through its pathways loved to roam,
     Sat beneath its pleasant shade,
But must hope that heav'nly bow'rs
May wear such hues as these of ours?

5

O ye fair and pleasant places,
     Where the eye, delighted, ranges;
O ye dear and friendly faces,
     Loved through all your mortal changes,
Are ye but stars, to shine through this life's night,
Doomed when the daylight beams to vanish from our sight?

Dreams

I   The Lilies

1

I dreamed that, from a low-walled mountain road,
I looked adown a long and dangerous steep,
Where 'mid rough stones and grass the waters flowed
Of a slow stream — so slow — it seemed to sleep.

2

Beside the rill a knot of flow'rs was growing
Like water-lilies, graceful, broad, and white;
Methought I clomb the wall, and fast was going
To pluck the lilies, fair and fresh and bright.

3

Downward, in spite of fear, my way I wound
To reach the spot whereon, it seemed, they grew:
But there arrived alas! I nothing found
Save mountain weeds of common form and line.

4

'Twas but a dream — yet ah! my soul, take heed
Lest such a dream thy waking hours portray.
How oft we hasten with but little speed
To gather blooms that vanish swift away!

5

The lilies blooming on the rough hill side
Are like vain wishes that my heart have cheated
Eager I've sought them, from afar descried,
But ah! ere I could reach them they have fleeted.

II   Time's Acquittal

1

I dreamed that, walking forth one summer's day
I chanced to meet old Time upon my way,
    And, full of spleen,
Taxed him with mischief he had done
To me and thousands more beneath the sun
    Plain to be seen.

2

'Blush, blush for shame', said I, 'to view this face
Despoiled by thee! – Canst thou one line retrace
   That erst was there?
I vow, ev'n I myself can scarce recall
It's heav'nly charm! – But I'm assured by all
   Old friends that it was fair.

3

'Come, thou canst bring it forth again, I know,
In pristine bloom – once more, ere yet I go
   Beneath the sod,
Present me to myself in finest feather
Of youth and health, – as when the mountain heather
     I lightly trod'.

4

Time seemed not all unwilling to comply:
Bade me look forth, and I should soon enjoy
   An apparition.
I looked: like morn slow-kindling in the skies
A dawn of rosy cheeks and sunny eyes
   Enriched my vision.

5

Cried I, 'This is the strangest thing on earth.
Two faces here I see – both full of mirth,
   And one much bolder
And broader too, like piony dispread,
Than mine, when wreathed in curls and garlanded,
   I looked no older'.

6

My children's faces! Time, I did thee wrong
Thou'st made me doubly blooming glad and strong! –
   Let my light wane –
Since stars new-ris'n my downward path are cheering
And for one radiance, now fast disappearing,
   Thou giv'st me twain.

III To a Friend

However dreams may be fallacious concerning outward events, yet may they be truly significant at home: and consolations or discouragements may be drawn from dreams which intimately tell us ourselves. Sir Thos. Browne.

To A. de Vere

Last night I had a troublous dream
De Vere I dreamt with pain of thee;
Methought the well-remembered stream
Of thy loved voice went rapidly
Beside me ever ever flowing,
But now not 'placid in its going',
No longer calm and clear and bright,
Suffused with Heav'n's serenest light:
The very sparkles and foamy spray,
The current flings up in its merriest play,
Pure as the still and silent snow,
That lies upon the mountain side;
By little rainbows glorified
Which stay while on the waters flow! –
Now all was changed – thy voice and look
Were such as I could scarcely brook.
'Twas thou and yet it was not thou, –
I gazed in fear and growing pain;
Thought's temple still was there – thy brow –
Thy gleaming eye, and yet 'twas plain,
That thou and Reason now were twain.

I ask not what this dream portends:
But wherefore was the vision sent?
For well I wot that Morpheus sends
Such dreams for our admonishment,
That we, by way of self-inspection,
May reach the goal of sage reflection.
It may be that with too much pride
I've thought, when thou wast by my side,
Or talked with tongue too bold and free
Of what thou art, and what to me.
Perhaps I've felt too proud and glad
That such a friend as thou I had,
Lowly-hearted yet high-minded,
Warm, but ne'er by passion blinded;

Full of fine poetic dreams
And philosophic inquisitions,
Careless of what the world esteems
Her low and profitless ambitions.
Yet apt for practice, – glad at heart
To take an unrewarded part,
To labour in Heav'ns hidden mine
Thy travail rather felt than known
And gather palms thy brow to twine
Seen by th'All-seeing Eyes alone! –
These lofty visions, hovering o'er me,
Have they displeased the Pow'rs of Night,
That thus my Friend was placed before me
Unclothed of Reason's holy light?

Ah no! the vision ne'er was sent
From vainer dreams my soul to free,
And bring me sadly to repent
Because I've deemed so well of thee.
I'll think 'twas sent to let me know
Through what mutations we may go
Of grievous loss or wondrous gain,
And yet our very selves remain.
I'll think that so shalt thou, my Friend,
As far thy present self transcend,
Reborn amid celestial light,
A last immortal changeless change,
As now thou dost to waking sight
That apparition sad and strange:
Thy fluent speech that sure must be
To those that, day by day, with thee
Live on, 'a dear domestic stream',
I see it glide with sunny gleam,
'Mid fields of bliss, to circle round
Bright meads of amaranthine flow'rs;
Thou image on its breast profound
Th'eternal City's glorious tow'rs.

Asceticism

Some teach that purity's high grace
Dwells but with those, who sternly chase
Each thought inspired by woman's face
    In all its modest splendour –
They bid you shun those timid eyes
Which can, at worst, but court surprise,
And when the wished pursuer flies
    Grow sad still more than tender.

Yet see how purest lilies grow –
What genial gales around them blow!
'Tis not 'mid chilling ice and snow
    They gain their snowy splendour;
Nor need ye seek a loftier strain
Of purity than he may gain
Who lives without one deeper stain
    Than what those looks engender.

O where shall bright-eyed Temperance go
And Modesty in vest of snow
Wearing upon her cheek the glow
    Of roses newly blown
If all the gifts of eye and ear
Our chastened senses can supply
Each soul that seeks the purest sky
    Must here on earth disown?

When Heav'n withdraws Life's summer breeze
Then – then 'tis time enough to freeze
Then Love's quick fire were but disease
    The hastener of our doom
True goodness pleased with Nature's plan –
To fill the sphere she marked for man,
Can calmly shrink into a span
    Then sink into the tomb.

Blanco White

Could'st thou in calmness yield thy mortal breath
Without the Christian's sure and certain hope?
Didst thou to earth confine our being's scope,
Yet, fixed on One Supreme with fervent faith,
Prompt to obey what conscience witnesseth
As one intent to fly th'eternal wrath
Decline the ways of sin that downward slope?
O thou light-searching spirit, that did'st grope
In such bleak shadows here, twixt life and death,
To thee dare I bear witness, though in ruth –
Brave witness like thine own – dare hope and pray
That thou, set free from this imprisoning clay,
Now clad in raiment of perpetual youth,
Mayst find that bliss untold, 'mid endless day,
Awaits each earnest soul that lives for Truth.

To a Friend who wished to give me half her sleep

No, gentle Friend, thou canst not give me sleep –
Yon velvet mead, that smiles beneath the steep,
Gives not its verdure to the soil-less rock –
Or when shall those bright clouds, Heav'n's countless flock,
With golden tissue line the chill sea-sand?
Or tempest-shattered trees, that pining stand
Receive rich robes, their nakedness to cover,
From leafy neighbours, blossom-starred all over?
If thou art Crœsus-rich in balmy slumbers,
As are thy waking hours in tuneful numbers,
Rich in Morphean poppies, richer still
In thoughts like roses, offspring of good will,
Thou shouldst be Dives with a wealthier heart,
Whilst I must wholly bear sad Lazarus' part,
Unless thy influence with the stars above
Should cause them on my head such dews to weep,
And pour such beams of their refreshing love
That, thus consoled, I scarce should pray for sleep.

To a Friend who prayed, that my heart might still be young

Reverse thy prayer, dear Friend, – no longer pray
That Time, who steals my outward youth away,
Should leave my heart still young, for in good sooth,
This heart, though sad, has all too much of youth –
I fain would find some marked mutations there
To match the altered eyes and cheeks and hair.

     The toys of childhood gladly are resigned,
Outgrown the childish form and childish mind:
But oh! the toys, the gauds of life's sweet prime
We scarce can yield to that base plund'rer Time.
Snowdrops and daffodils may pass away,
Violet and harebell, sweeter far than they,
Will soon be here, with blossoms of the May:
And promises 'moon-lighted all day long'
When Summer comes, with her sun-radiant throng,
May die forsaken – but June's glowing roses,
We ill can hear that *they* should 'have their closes',
And mutely weep, 'mid Autumn's mellow store,
Because the soft flow'r-meteors shine no more.

     Love is the fairest toy that earth can give –
Bright play-thing – yet the bread whereon we live!
And many a hand essays that toy to hold
With grasp, too youthful eager, yet too old.
Thine eyes, Philario, once could love inspire,
But Time's sure hand has stol'n their potent fire:
Then seek no more with stealthy desp'rate aim
To seize Love's quiver and secure his flame,
Lest, foiled and wounded, thou should'st sigh to find,
That Love is ever wakeful and *not* blind.

On reading my Father's 'Youth and Age'

Sometimes 'tis with a touch of natural grief
That I behold the sere and yellow leaf
I'm fallen into – my summer scarce yet gone,
When th'year should put some solid bravery on:
And think that, had the skies been less unkind,
Nor sent an untimely frost and winter wind
Into my Autumn, it might well have shown
A verdure and luxuriance of its own,
Somewhat more answering to my vernal hour,
When, spite of many a blast and beating show'r,
Not much I lacked of Spring's enchanting dow'r.
    But soon some better thoughts I hope to win
I ask, what aspect wears the soul within?
In her do those, who clearest see, descry
The wasted form, wan cheek and sunken eye?
Or hath she put some Autumn bravery on
To recompense for Spring and Summer gone,
And, 'mid the cruel season's wasting stress,
More gained in pow'r than lost in loveliness?
To this my gentle friends shall answer make:
Their thoughts thereon I'll gladly take
For my soul's mirror, and will strive to be
Whate'er that flatt'ring glass reports of me.
This only dare I for myself to say,
That, let me lose or gain what charms I may,
Heav'n grants me more and more a heart t'admire
All beauty that can genial thoughts inspire.
And though this truth no genuine sage assails,
'Less what we *have* than what we *are* avails',
Herein *to have* is surely best by far –
To – gaze – to love – and care not what we *are*.

To a little weanling Babe, who returned a kiss with great eagerness

Pretty Babe, 'tis all in vain,
Thou may'st suck and suck again,
But the lip, though soft it be,
Is no fount of milk for thee.
Baby, no! 'tis soft as silk,
Yet has nought to do with milk;
From the banks, where roses grow,
Lily streams shall never flow.

Baby when at man's estate,
Thou, with youthful hopes elate,
Seekest all things else above
Lady's fluent words of love;
Ne'er may lip, whence oft, in dreams,
Flow for thee those nectar streams,
Dry as bloomless desart prove
When thou askest love for love.

Dream-love

The union of thy heart and mine,
Ah yes! I know 'tis all a dream:
For I am dark, in life's decline –
Round thee the noon-day splendours beam:
But let this fair tho' flickering gleam
Of fancied love one moment shine;
Thou mayst afford at least to seem
For one brief moment to be mine.

Haste not at once to break the spell –
Before thee is the long long day
With gayer hearts than mine to dwell,
In laughing meads far off to stray:
One little hour beside me stay,
And let the conscious dream go on;
E'en now the tears are on their way
To flood my cheeks when thou art gone.

More brightness than is wholly thine
Will vanish with thy last adieu,
For whilst I dream that thou art mine
It seems my youth is with me too;
My glittering youth thy looks renew,
That turned on me so brightly beam,
As if from mine fresh light they drew –
Of light and love is all my dream.

Can dream-light to the soul be dear?
Ah! who would weep, 'mid light of day,
To see the meteors disappear,
'The cold phosphoric fires decay'?
But when my dream-light fades away
What darkness will my soul invade? –
For sunshine or the moon's mild ray
One mass of cheerless, starless shade.

Fade phantom dream-light, full of strife,
Oh fade before that serious mien,
Which, kind and warm as day and life,
Is e'en as painless death serene.
The storm-clouds 'mid the radiance keen
Of Heav'n's deep vault how lost are they! –
So might I 'mid the azure sheen
Of that pure spirit melt away!

To my Son

Love to admire – avoid depreciation –
Base is that alchemy which turns pure gold
To copper in the servile estimation
Of men who but with others' eyes behold, –
Who seek the brightest things to dull and tarnish,
Dull stuff of their own mint to brighten up and varnish.

Love to admire – the sun at noon-day blazing
Blasts the beholder's eye with light intense:
But sun-bright excellence rewards our gazing,
Imparts new vigour to the inward sense.
Wish to admire, to love, to hope, believe,
All that thou hopest, lov'st, thou shalt in time receive.

Th'admirer all that he admires possesses –
Unnumbered treasures for his treasury hath:
Is owner of a thousand gifts and graces,
Which are but thorns in Envy's painful path:
Resides in an Elysian summer calm
While round his happy head blow countless gales of balm.

Some men there are, who deal in moderation
Only to gratify immoderate spite:
Make a man's obvious virtues a firm station,
Whence they take aim to fetch him from his height;
They grant a little to deprive of much,
And numb the gen'rous heat with their torpedo touch.

Dread not an argument, but bravely say
'Tis victory by truth to be subdued;
But, if thy tongue and not thy mind gives way,
Then bear the victor's scoff with fortitude:
View it as martyrdom for truth's dear sake,
A mild refining fire and temper's easy stake.

Dread not a laugh – contemn th' unmeaning sneer
Of men who with no finer sword can fence. –
A laugh, the last thing we learn not to fear,
Is oft the dullard's substitute for sense.
Laugh thou when Pride and feeble Mimicry
Seize Mirth's gay mask and wear it all awry.

True irony is but a form of reason,
An argument in gala clothing drest, –
But they who breathe March winds in summer season, –
And vent mere rancour in the form of jest,
Deserve no credit in their serious vein.
Their earnest is a jest which merits but disdain.

How oft we grieve that a friend's inward wealth
Of small account by loveless crowds is made!
Yet who seek glory from their strength and health,
Or pine to have their heavy coffers weighed?
They that possess, the inward jewel, worth
Have present heav'n within and gain thereto th' earth.

For not beneath the light of common day,
And not to eyes by common beams enlightened,
That jewel doth its brilliant hues display:
'Tis by an inward luminary brightened;
And they who those pure beams participate
Alone can see that fair which they illuminate.

Goodness is never perfect in one mind,
But widely o'er the earth in parcels spread:
As gold, in fragments to the streams consigned,
Was ne'er discovered in its mountain bed,
So hope not thou, ere from this earth ascended,
To find all virtues in one mortal mansion blended.

Yet some all moral good and evil find in masses
Which no opposing quality doth leaven:
Mankind at large they place in two large classes
The heavenly – and the sort devoid of heav'n –
Sure they see double in their partial kindness
For Virtue on one side have nought but total blindness.

Learn to be true, for 'tis consummate art
From all untruth our thoughts, words, acts to clear: –
Detect the falsehoods of the cunning heart,
Which least of all is with itself sincere:
Small need hast thou with others to eschew
The base deceiver's way while thou to self art true.

Tennyson's 'Lotos Eaters' with a new conclusion

'The Lotos blooms below the flowery peak:
The Lotos blows by every winding creek:
All day the wind breathes low with mellower tone:
Thro' every hollow cave and alley lone
Round and round the spicy downs the yellow Lotos-dust is blown.
We have had enough of motion,
Weariness and wild alarms,
Tossing on the restless Ocean',

Here are a thousand charms,
One best of all, that every pang disarms,
Th'enchanted lotos bloom o'er all our senses reigning
'Then lift no more the shattered oar,
No more unfurl the straining sail.'
We will abide in the golden vale
One radiant smile our trancèd gaze detaining
Of one calm lake out of whose bosom ever,
Drawn from many a shadowy fountain,
In yon far distant boundary mountain
Softly flows the travelled river
Just heard above the stock dove's plaining:
Or, borne upon the wave, with lilies float,
Tranquil as they amid the slumb'rous gleam,
Or, in the zephyr-wafted boat,
As though we flew unpinioned in a dream
From fragrant bank to bank pass lightly o'er.
'Hark how sweet the horned ewes bleat
On the solitary steeps
And the merry lizard leaps
And the foam white waters pour:
And the dark pine weeps,
And the lithe vine creeps,
And the heavy melon sleeps
On the level of the shore:
Oh islanders of Ithaca we will not wander more.'

'We have had enough of motion,
Weariness and wild alarm,
Tossing on the restless ocean,'
'Long enough the wine-dark wave our weary bark did carry.'
Here are a thousand charms
One best of all that every pang disarms,
The Lotos-bloom that woos us in the vale to tarry.

We will abide in the golden vale
And never launch into the boundless plain,
The watery waste where threat'ning billows roar,
But nigh the sapphire lake remain
In whose deep hospitable breast
Derived from many a shadowy fountain
In yon far distant sky-commingled mountain
The travelled waters sink to rest,
And there beside th'untroubled lilies float.

Crashaw's Poetry

Heav'ns what a load of soft rich beamy things,
Crashaw, streams forth from thy poetic fount! –
How thy bright Muse on her bespangled wings
Quivers and glitters o'er the Roman Mount! –
How doth she fling abroad with hand profuse
Flow'rs of all hue and fruits of every juice,
Oil, milk and honey, nect'rous wines and spices,
     Culled from 'ten thousand thousand Paradises',
Delicious dews and dulcet creams,
Soft sleeps ambrosial and ecstatic dreams,
     The raptured vision
That steeps the soul in bliss Elysian
And wraps it in the splendour of [? blessèd-heavenly] beams.

    Purple rivers, 'blubbering mountains',★
    Balm and nectar bubbling fountains,
    Fruits from laden boughs that dangle
    In the greenwood's verdant tangle,
All these she joins in 'silver-sweating streams'.★★
                Nor lacks she jewels rare
Bright gemmy tear-drops, and bright tearlike gems,
Roses that blush upon their bloomy stems,
And lilies that o'erload with balm the fainting air.
   But best of all she loves, when cares molest,
The 'spicy', 'perfumed', 'gorgeous', 'virgin nest',
In which her 'unfledged griefs' may take their rest,
The tender turtle-dove's poor 'panting breast'
'Swoln rhapsodies' and raptures unexprest
And 'flash of highborn fancies' far beyond compare.
   'Delicious death, soft exhalations
   Of soul, dear and divine annihilations',
   Empurpled transports, golden blisses,
   Inebriating wildernesses
Of 'rarefied delights', red hopes and 'bloomy joys',
Far from the vain tumultuous 'shops of noise'
Too mystically bright for such a world as this is. –

    'Amorous languishments, luminous trances',
    Pure and subtle lightning glances,
    Which set the spirit's house on fire,
    Yea melt it down, into a liquid form,

Then simmer it away★★★ 'mid flames that high aspire
Till forth it flows the polar seas to warm −
Labyrinths of tangled pleasures★★★★
Which the carnal worldling misses,
'Boundless and infinite bottomless treasures',
Which travel down the soul's abysses,
Immortal amaranthine kisses
From lips which forty thousand 'roseal springs'
With bloom and fragrancy not over-furnish,
Cheeks, whose refulgent hues might serve to burnish
Morn's glowing portals − all resplendent things,
  Of every sort and kind,
  Which make the gazer blind,
And weigh with glory down the spirit's wings,
Thrillings and trillings and delicate quaverings
Songs seraphic and symphonies grand
Wafting of wings and wavings and waverings,
Over the sea and over the land,
All with a swimming tumultuous motion
Mingle in Crashaw's poetical Ocean.

★I have seen Helm Crag blubber dreadfully after heavy rains.
★★ I wish that streams would have retained this good habit to the present day and
 help one to pay the income tax.
★★★ Or clarify it off − a metaphor taken from the preserving pan.
★★★★Refined pleasures grow so thick in the well-cultured soul that their branches
 become interlaced.

'On the same'

Nectar, nectar everywhere, but not a drop to drink
Of pure and purifying streams that in the spirit sink: −
Beams and flashes everywhere but ne'er a little blink
Of Reason's strong and steady light, which leads the heart to think.

'Toil not for burnished gold that poorly shines,'

Let me have noble toils, if toil I must,
The Patriot's task or Friendship's sacred cares.

A. de Vere

Cur valle permutem Sabina
Divitias operosiores?

Horace

1

Toil not for burnished gold that poorly shines,
Whilst the soul rusts and her pure life declines;
Nor Honour's purple robe, that but constrains
Full many a wight that wears it for his pains;
Nor treacherous Fame that oft defames in praising,
Nor fairest face that fades whilst thou art gazing,
Like evening clouds, now filled with rosy light
Now dull as lead beneath the brow of Night: –
But labour lest thy spirit be opprest
With unfilled leisure – that supreme unrest –
Worst load that life can lay upon a mortal breast.

2

What are professions? Means to gather wealth
At risk of conscience, comfort, calmness, health? –
Nay, view them in their larger nobler plan
As social services of man to man.
Labour for wealth – to use at God's command,
And spread his blessings over sea and land;
For pow'r and influence, that thy Christian soul,
Cased in strong mail, may conquer and control;
Labour in youth, that when 'grey hairs are nigh',
Thy youthful 'thoughts and feelings may not die',
While no new fount springs up to bring a fresh supply.

3

Toil not for Earth's 'low things' as for an end
Tow'rd which thy hopes and aims conveying tend; –
But work that thou may'st fill the largest sphere
Assigned by Heav'n to man's existence here.
Soft dreams, mild cares those manly sinews melt
That for strong ends and strenuous means were dealt.
Pow'rs by inaction shrink – they need the strain
Of some great purpose, fitted to retain
Its place as Life's main beam, round which entwined
The soft light wreaths may hang at will combined. –
Begin! – for soon the evening clouds descend,
Slackening our hands, that fain their work would mend,
And lo then cometh Night, which all our work must end.

Sketch from Life. Morning Scene. Sept 22 1845

Great part of last night, like 'a windladen billow',
I tossed to and fro on my slumberless pillow:
At last when Aurora appeared in the sky,
And on me cast down a compassionate eye
God Somnus, to please her, stretched over my head
His word of repose and I lay as one dead,
Or still as a vessel that strikes on a rock,
And after long tossing receives her last shock.
But scarce half an hour had I calmly respired
When in came my boy with his countenance fired,
And stood by my bed with a theme in his hand
Determined my wakefullest thoughts to command.

A Boy's complaint of Dr Blimber

Cried he in a tone of despair, may I die,
If to please the old Grinder I ever more try:
His scores and his scratches no fellow can bear;
This excellent theme all to pieces I'll tear.
Corrections he makes just to show his red ink,
For no other object – and what do you think?
A passage he marks with his disapprobations
I took from Mark Tully's most classic oration!
If he can improve upon Cicero's style
Such news I han't heard for a very long while;
But all who have brains in their skulls must agree
Such talent can ne'er be expected of me.

L'Envoy to 'Phantasmion'

Go, little book, and sing of love and beauty,
To tempt the worldling into fairy land:
Tell him that airy dreams are sacred duty,
Bring better wealth than aught his toils command
    Toils fraught with mickle harm.

But if thou meet some spirit high and tender
On blessed works and noblest love intent:
Tell *him* that airy dreams of Nature's splendour,
With graver thoughts and hallowed musings blent,
    Prove no too earthly charm.

Feydeleen to Zelneth

Fair maid, yield not thy soul to gloom,
Nor that soft cheek to Sorrow's pow'r;
If he looks coldly on thy bloom
Must thou become a withered flow'r?

He cannot love: – yet thou art fair;
The fault is wholly his, not thine;
How great his folly all shall swear,
That see thy charms serenely shine.

When beaming beauty beams in vain,
And fails to melt the frozen heart,
The wound is sharp, yet heals amain;
Love leaves her still his better part.

But hers is no such passing pain,
Who loves when lovely youth is fled:
And feels that not e'en love to gain
Could raise her beauty from the dead:

Who hears the wind that courts the trees
Thus whisp'ring mock her hopeless grief;
'When e'er did Love's soft summer breeze
Caress the sere and yellow leaf?'

Song of Leucoia

O had I love-inspiring eyes
As brightly blue as summer skies:
Rich locks flowing wave on wave,
Lips 'whose hue, angry and brave'
Makes the rose less fair to see,
A form of finest symmetry,
Such as angels wear above, –
Then, then I'd pray to be thy love.

O were I of a home possest
Like fabled islands of the blest,
Where nobler woods and purer streams,
And meads enriched with gladder beams
Than earth can boast or poets feign,
Outshone the gold of Saturn's reign,
I'd pray the gods on bended knee
That thou might'st share that home with me.

But ah! my looks are dim and wan
As flow'rs when evening shades come on:
For Hope, that on my heart lies dead
Her deathy hue hath round her spread;
And Love's deep glow within my heart
Is imaged in no outward part: –
I'd rather Night should wed with Day
Than thou in my dull shadow stay.

Nor hath this earth a spot so fair
That I could wish thy home were there;
Better in dreams to have thee mine
Than here where suns so feeble shine:
In heaven thy blissful seat provide,
Myself a spirit by thy side,
And Love's glad prospect never-ending
Its mazes in our sight extending.

Song for 'Phantasmion'

1

Ere I loved thee what hue did the May blossoms wear,
And how were the rose and the woodbine attired:
When the notes of the nightingale floated in air,
Did I list to the music as if 'twere inspired? –
I ask not blest Lover – nor seek to recall
That season of dimness and winterly cold;
The sun is now shining – it shines over all,
And all things are painted with purple and gold.

2

Were the sun of my love blotted out from the sky,
How then would the rose and the woodbine appear?
When the lark sang his song as he mounted on high,
How then would his melody sound in mine ear? –
Full surely I know not: my seasons would fail,
Could I truly depicture that blackness and gloom:
Ere it comes may this joy-illumed cheek have grown pale,
And dark with the shadows that fall from the tomb.

Zelneth. Love unreturned

Thine eyes are kindly bent on mine,
Their gentle glance I scarce can bear:
It bids me every hope resign,
It fills my soul with deep despair.
Alas! that look so kind, so calm, so free
Tells me thou lovest not as I love thee.

When thou'rt afar I see thy face;
Before me still it softly gleams;
The vision has not half thy grace,
I cannot paint thee in my dreams:
Yet ah! dear face, would'st thou but gaze on me
With such a look as in those dreams I see.

The vision changes in my sight,
No more it looks as I am feeling;
'Twas Hope lit up that sunny light
A lover's full glad heart revealing;
Hope joined with Love to frame that vision fair;
Now Love's bright work is shadowed by Despair.

Then bend thine eyes no more on mine,
Since love alone those looks inspire,
Those looks with their soft sunny shine
Kindle a sharp consuming fire,
And, while they glow with Hope and youthful glee,
Silence each pulse of Hope that beats in me.

Matthew VI.28–9

Behold the lilies of the field
   Arrayed beyond compare!
No loom on earth did ever yield
   A tissue half so fair:
No rich and splendid potentate
   Was e'er so well attired;
It seems as tho' their bloomy state
   Was made to be admired.

The lilies neither spin nor weave,
   But Nature's laws obey,
And thus from Nature's Lord receive
   Their garments fair and gay:
And we if by His will we live,
   May cast our cares aside,
Secure that He our bread will give
   And raiment meet provide.

But tho' the lilies in their bloom
    So gloriously are drest,
That broid'ress hand and weaver's loom
    Ne'er framed so fine a vest,
Yet far more glorious robes than these
    Our Saviour doth prepare
For souls, that seek their God to please,
    In Heav'n's bright courts to wear.

Yes! He, in his almighty love,
    Prepares the raiment fine,
That souls shall wear in Heav'n above,
    Illumed with light divine;
Yet we ourselves must labour too,
    Assisted by this grace,
Our souls in raiment to endue
    Meet for a holier place.

E'en here below that clothing bright,
    The Heav'n-born souls array,
Shines with a steady inward light
    As clear as light of day:
Fairer than flow'rs that deck the mead
    To Faith's keen sight revealed,
To worldly eyes a beggar's weed,
    Its splendours all concealed.

The robes, in which the souls that live
    Before their God appear,
Though Christ the rich material give,
    Are framed and fashioned here:
If here in earth's low shadowy vale
    Those robes like glow-worms gleam,
They'll make the glittering stars look pale
    When high in Heav'n they beam.

Prayer for Tranquillity

Dear Lord, who, at thy blessed will,
Could'st make the raging wind be still,
And smooth the tossing of the sea
Oh cause our stormy griefs to flee,
Our wild tumultuous thoughts allay
And tempest passions send away:
Conduct us here to perfect peace,
Where all our earthly troubles cease
And lastly, while to Thee we cling,
Our souls to that blest haven bring,
Above the sphere of Care and Woe,
Where earthly blasts can never blow,
With Thee to dwell, supremely blest,
Anchored on everlasting Rest.

The melancholy Prince

I see the sun rise while the shadows are waning,
But darkness alone in my spirit is reigning;
The Rivers are glad once again to be clad
In the rich golden light that he scatters around,
And with voices of pleasure the forests resound –
Ah! why do these visages, hideous and black,
Still frown upon me tho' the sun is come back?

The waters of Pleasure beside me are sweeping,
As fast as they flow all as fast am I weeping;
No drop do I taste while my hours run to waste,
For to me they are bitter as tears that I shed
And alas! it were fitter to lay down my head,
And to sink in the Earth, like the soft summer rain,
Than to gaze on the waters of Pleasure in vain.

I roam in the glades of the Forest alone:
The trees of my garden unlovely are grown:
But far as I range I can meet with no change;
A mist from within comes to darken my sight,
And rests on the landscape like fog or a blight –
Wan, frigid and cheerless all nature is seen,
Like hoar-frosted meadows despoiled of their green.

I envy the beasts that are seeking their prey,
And the vile slimy reptile that crawls in my way;
Yon carolling bird makes his joy to be heard –
Ah! now he is falling! – he carols no more! –
His shouting and singing and soaring are o'er! –
Yet I envy him still, as he falls on his nest,
With the sharp-pointed arrow stuck deep in his breast.

Zelneth's Song in Magnart's Garden

1

When smiling skies unkindly grow
The stricken streams, forbid to flow,
No more that faithless heaven reflect
Which all their sparkling mirth has checked,
Be thou, my heart, like frozen streams,
Since Love for thee no longer beams;
Oh! let thy trembling motion sleep,
Nor still one treach'rous image keep.

2

These tender flowers, now Eve draws on,
Though wide dispread in light they shone,
Like drowsy eyes by slumber prest,
Slow folding nod in dewy rest.
But I, a rose too quickly blown,
Must fall, hue, form and fragrance flown;
This heart, once opened, ne'er can close,
Ne'er find, in Love's chill night, repose.

The garden's pride, that blooms so bright,
    When rills are dancing,
Spreads not a petal to the light
    From snow plains glancing:
Ah! lavish rose, why all bestow
    On summer breezes? –
Away to find fresh flow'rs *they* go,
    When here it freezes.

Children

1

When little children weep we smile upon their tears,
And a truer, brighter smile on the dewy face appears;
Oh! Grief that comes so fast and makes so little stay,
Is like the snow of Springtide, which falls to melt away.

2

The happy Shepherd's flute across the Lake we hear,
And love the softened sound more than music full and clear –
Content with scattered notes of that far distant strain,
We ask not of the melody to trace its mazy chain.

3

And oh! how small a part do childish minds descry
Of all that complex world, which they view with gladdened eye!
Nor need they yet combine the forms and hues of earth,
Each in itself hath charms for them and all sufficient worth.

4

But children have their sorrow, for Fancy does them wrong
And binds the unresisting soul with fetters hard and strong;
(They see the gloomy sky nor know 'tis here decreed
That sunshine follow every storm and light to shade succeed).

5

The outward show of things these little ones behold,
And when their heart is warm all they look upon is gold;
But when the spirit flags while the tapers dimly burn,
They see not how it goes, nor how it may return.

6

I love thee little brother when smiles are on thy face, –
Thy child-like perfect merriment and never-failing grace:
But when the shadow darkens thee and chills thy timid breast,
I'd watch from eve till daybreak that thou mightst be at rest.

7

I dread the ghastly witch and the goblin of the dark,
And often shrink with fear till the singing of the lark;
But pity makes us bold, and to hide them, dear, from thee,
I'd stand and face them steadfastly till morning bids them flee.

8

Come listen to my voice while I tell thee of a land,
Where thou and I will dwell with a merry merry band;
Where darkness never falls on the meadows gay and bright,
Except the pleasant shadow all islanded in light.

'Passion is blind not Love: her *wondrous might'*

*These few lines are an attempt to bring out a sentiment, which my Father once
expressed to me on the common saying that 'Love is blind'.*

Passion is blind not Love: *her* wondrous might
Informs with three-fold pow'r man's inward sight: –
To her deep glance the soul at large displayed
Shews all its mingled mass of light and shade: –
Men call her blind when she but turns her head,
Nor scans the fault for which her tears are shed.
Can dull Indifference or Hate's troubled gaze
See through the secret heart's mysterious maze? –

Can Scorn and Envy pierce that 'dread abode',
Where true faults rest beneath the eye of God?
Not theirs, 'mid inward darkness, to discern
The spiritual splendours how they shine and burn.
All bright endowments of a noble mind
They, who with joy behold them, soonest find;
And better none its stains of frailty know
Than they who fain would see it white as snow.

'O change that strain with man's best hopes at strife,'

'The grey-haired Saint may fail at last,
The surest guide a wanderer prove:
Death only binds us fast
To the bright shore of Love.'
from *The Christian Year*

O change that strain with man's best hopes at strife,
    A recreant strain that wrongs the steadfast soul!
    Vainly against that bark the billows roll,
Which bears within the Eternal Lord of Life.

Bright sparks ay glitter, – flames may mount on high
    In quick warm hearts, yet faithless, – then expire:
    But God can kindle in the soul a fire
Of force t'outlive yon Sun that lights the sky.

Can he be meet to dwell with Saints above,
    And gaze upon his Saviour face to face,
    Who might, were life prolonged, abandon grace,
And madly trample on redeeming love?

Does God bind some to that bright heav'nly shore,
    Who here on earth might wander from His way;
    And banish others from Eternal Day,
Who might return to paths of peace once more?

Does Heav'n decide our fate for weal or woe,
    Not we ourselves by choice of good or ill;
    Unfailing choice, persistency of will,
In Christ to live, or sink with fiends below?

Just heav'n forefend! Eternal joys or pains,
    These wait on man by man's own changeless choice:
    And God proclaims with no uncertain voice
His Sons are they in whom His seed *remains.*

The Saviour knows the saved; – those sheep discerns
    Who ne'er shall wander from His careful hand;
    He knows the sp'rits that shall for ever stand,
The calm bright cells where fire perpetual burns!

Then, gentle Harmonist, that strain forebear;
    Oh! cast not out from joy the faithful heart!
    Firmly they choose who gain the better part,
And ev'n in time eternal blessings share.

Heav'n even here surrounds the filial breast,
    Even here our earthly cares and troubles cease.
    And what were *heav'n* without a *settled* peace, –
Has He not promised His beloved rest?

'O vain expenditure! unhallowed waste!'

O vain expenditure! unhallowed waste!
Thus to bestow on the swathed infant heir
Full flowing robes, too large for him to wear! –
On his frail head, as if in mockery, placed
That crown with which the ample brows are graced
Of saints who, proud their Saviour's cross to bear,
His blessed steps pursue with ceaseless care,
Through arduous ways to do His bidding haste!
Why should we give to the close-folded rose
Those glowing tints that glad the gazer's eye?
Soon shall it brightly blossom where it grows;
Or, if at once transported to the sky,
Such colours in that temperature disclose
As here e'en light from heaven could ne'er supply.

The Infant soul is as a frozen lake,
O'er which Heav'n smiles and playful breezes stray;
It cannot smile as yet, nor lightly play,
Nor of the skies one soft bright image take.
But soon the slumbering waters are awake,
Released from durance by the kindly ray;
Then see it laugh beneath the eye of Day!
Its lapsing bosom every breath can shake,
Unconsciousness, our spirits' primal frost,
Yields, 'sure as day to night', to Pow'r supreme:
How unlike that which not the fervid beam
Of Love can melt, in souls for ever lost! –
Amid that genial warmth self-frozen – grown
No transient ice but undissolving stone!

Darling Edith

Darling little Sister Edith
Little knoweth little heedeth,
Little hath and little needeth
   Little hath to fear;
Easy is the life she leadeth
   Life without a tear.

See her soon a busier Edith:
Book and pen and pencil needeth:
Many a pretty lesson readeth
   To her mother dear;
Still an easy life she leadeth
   Life without a tear.

Now she's grown an older Edith
Now how much she knoweth, heedeth,
Thinking oft of him that needeth
   With a heart sincere! –
By the gentle life she leadeth
   Drying many a tear.

First chorus in 'The Agamemnon' of Æschylus

'Tis the tenth year since adversaries dread
To Priam, they who from high Jove obtain
Twin-sceptred and twin-throned to reign,
Great Sons of Atreus, famed for hardyhead,
A military force for vengeance led,
Freight of a thousand vessels, from this shore
Pouring from their bold breasts a mighty shout of war;
Like Vultures that around their nest on high
Smit by the loss of young with sharpest pain
  In agitated circles fly,
And, whilst they ply aloft the plumy oar,
With their shrill sorrows pierce the quiet sky
For long long brooding cares and labour spent in vain.
  But from his high domain
 Some retributive Pow'r that dwells above,
 Apollo, Pan, or all perfecting Jove
  Struck by the clamorous lament
 Of these wild wanderers from a plundered home,
 'Gainst the transgressors, wheresoe'er they roam,
 Sends an avenging Fury, sure though late.

Thus against Paris in his ire
Jove, God of hospitable rites, hath sent
Th'Atridæ to be ministers of Fate: –
  Wrestlings many and dire
 All for a double-mated woman,
 Both on Greek and Trojan foeman
 Imposing – ah! how many a knee
 Propped on the dust! what snapping, shivering
 Of spears in the crash of onset! – what a quivering
  Of limbs o'erlaboured in death's agony!

But come what may, beneath the sun
All that on high is destined shall be done:
 For not by streams of sacrifice
 Nor tears that gush from downcast eyes,
 Nor hands upraised, mid supplicating cries,
  A mortal man's impiety
The wrath of righteous Heaven may ever hope to shun.

But we, from that great armament omitted,
    Alas! unfitted
For battle deeds, must here abide
    To second childhood grown
Leaning upon a staff our weary gait to guide.
    For when glad youth is flown,
Its fires extinct, its vigorous juices dried,
Ah! then how perishes the pride
Of our green summer foliage! – then we feebly stray
    On three feet weeping, and with waste of years
      Frail as a child the man appears –
A pale and fleeting dream by the sun's light espied.

But say, O child of Tyndarus, our Queen,
What may this sudden splendour mean?
What message coming to thine ears this day
Has stirred thy spirit with a glad surprise
That thus in joy's triumphant way
Thou sendest all about to sacrifice?
What, Clytemnestra, hast thou heard, what fame
Has caused thee to light up this general flame?

    See all around
Of every guardian Deity
That rules within the city's bound,
Earthly or heavenly, which soe'er he be,
Yea and of each bright company
    O'er the Forum here presiding,
    Or in realms above residing,
      With gifts the hallowed altars blaze.

On this side and on that a torch of fire,
A glittering torch the sacred hearths upraise;
    Behold what unctuous fomentations,
    With fragrant incense fraught,
    What masses from the inner chambers brought
      Of clotted oil, rich royal preparations,
      Feed those keen flames that to the skies aspire!

Speak and of these things tell us whatsoe'er
    Thou canst and mayst declare:
O be the healer of solicitude,
Which now o'erclouds our hearts with sadness

Now, while those fires, around us shining,
  Betoken gladness
Gives place to Hope that hastes in joyous mood
  To banish soul-consuming Care,
  Of grief insatiate, with her blest divining.

Poems written for a book of Dialogues on the Doctrines of grace

I

While disputants for victory fight,
And hope to fill the world with light,
Enkindled from Truth's piercing ray,
She, prudent Virgin, steals away,
Swift hastens off with shrouded lamp,
And dark'ling leaves the noisy camp.

Eftsoon she gains a silent dell
Where Peace and Meditation dwell,
Where no rude gales contending blow,
But fires of deep Devotion glow,
There feeds and fans her sacred flame,
Still growing, yet for aye the same.

II
Water can but rise to its own level

Think not by laboured proof or plea profound
Vain minds to free from superstitions vain,
Or snap one link of Error's unfelt chain,
Which Time aye winds the careless spirit around:
If cheated into Faith by shew of Reason,
And Sophistry's assumptions broad and bold,
From *Thought* they had received the creed they hold
With unrelaxing grasp, at some fit season,
Thought's sovereign might find access to their mind,
Fair Truth, by Candour led, with open face,
And listening to her voice, thro' Heaven's high grace,
By *Thought* they might those subtle bands unbind;

Might learn how Falsehood coins her counters base,
And change them for pure metal twice refined.

III
Reason

That ancient hero, Theseus hight,
Had he disdained the proffered aid
Of Ariadne, gracious Maid,
Whose star hath since illumed the night,
For all his wondrous hardihood,
And all his matchless skill at arms,
Had never freed from dire alarms
Fair Athens, and her Foe subdued;
Nor saved her youthful children from their fate,
But perished in those windings intricate.

We too a labyrinth have to tread,
Where uncouth monstrous forms abide,
And we too have as sure a Guide
As that by which his steps were led:
Our Ariadne, kind and true,
Than she of old more brightly fair –
Reason – doth our escape prepare,
And places in our hands a clue:
Her armour guards us in all dang'rous frays,
Her lamp around us sheds its piercing rays,
Whilst on we fare thru' Error's shadowy maze.

IV
Mystic Doctrine of Baptism

We read of a mad enterprise
    In Holy Writ,
Of men who sought to gain the skies
    By their own wit:
How God's abode they strove to reach
    By Him untaught,
Till strange confusion on their speech
    Th' Almighty brought;
And how that structure, impotent and vain,
Was left for aye unfinished on the plain.

Thus false Theology her tow'r
    Of Babel rears,
To last, by human skill and pow'r,
    For endless years;
And shews a way to Heav'n above
    Of her own framing;
But He, the Lord of Light and Love,
    Her work disclaiming,
Reveals it for a fabric of delusion,
In darkness founded, ending in confusion.

Smit by His beams the mazy pile
    Dissolves in air:
But lo! Beneath Heav'n's radiant smile
    A structure fair! –
Deep in the heart of man was cast
    Its broad foundation
More glorious each day than the last
    It keeps its station: –
This is the gradual stair sublime
    The golden stair to heaven,
    By Truth and Mercy given,
Knowledge, Faith, Hope and Love, by which to God we climb!

V
Baptism

If ye were raised with Christ, go seek your treasure
Where He abides, and quit this Earth's dull prison;
Leave the vile body of low sensuous pleasure
Fixed on the cross, and be in spirit arisen.

If light from heaven have beamed upon your way,
Walk in those beams beneath the broad blue dome:
Shun Earth's false fires that shine but to betray,
Nor dare thro' Error's darksome tracts to roam.

Quickened with Christ in that life-giving stream,
His life to live be aye your soul's endeavour:
Think this world's pageant but a passing dream,
Nor slumber here but watch to wake for ever.

[Verses from 'Regeneration']

This is a giddy world of chance and changing
But none shall reign in life with Christ above
Whose souls are not secured from sinful ranging
Anchored for aye on Christian faith and love.

For He o'ercame the world
That faith which brings us into life eternal
That love which fits us in His sight to dwell
Can never yield   supernal

Missionary Poem

A wanderer lost 'mid parching sands
Beneath Zahara's torrid sky
Lifts in despair his wasted hands
No longed for well, no shelter nigh;
When lo he stands mid sylvan shades –
Some Power benign has changed the scene:
Beneath the leaves fresh fountains play
And cattle stray o'er pastures green.

The victim of some fell disease
That daily blurs fair nature's plan,
Robs life of every pow'r to please
And fills with woe a shortened span –
What joy is his, when, swift as light,
From wasted limbs the shackles fall,
Bright day succeeds to spectral night,
And festive robe to funeral pall!

O happy man but far more [?blest] is he
To whom the Gospel first is given
Who hears of life and immortality
Promised to men by messages from heaven
Ah far more glorious change more bliss
From death to life and the glad Gospels real fruition

[From Sara Coleridge's Journal, September 1850]

I must here preserve my opinion on a young lady's assertion that she had danced forty times at a Plymouth ball.

> Danced forty times? We know full well
>   That earthly balls are not eternal:
> Still oftener perhaps in hell
>   You'll whirl away in a waltz infernal.

Another.

> Danced forty times? What ne'er give o'er
> But keep possession of the floor,
> The silly wall-flowers round you pining, –
> Rejected swains for envy whining! –

> Perpetual motion's quite entrancing
> With angel partners bright and clever
> But sure with thee a whole nights dancing
> Would make the wretch lie still for ever.

> Danced forty times? Is Plymouth town
>   Disfurnished then of bonny lasses?
> Danced forty times? Is Plymouth town
>   Become a wilderness of asses?

'Tis all a trifle in words and upon paper, but I have been long married, and know what intricately unrememberable stuff it is that makes up misery!

[From a letter to Mrs Derwent Coleridge, 16 January 1852]

> Sing hey diddle diddle,
> The Cat and the Fiddle,
>   I've found my *Lloyd and Lamb*!!!
> The Moschus and Bion
> I can't yet set eye on,
>   But 'tother is worth a fat Ram!
>   Lloyd and Lamb –
>   (How happy I am!) –
> Together with Coleridge are worth a fat Ram.

Sing hey diddle doxon
That good Mr Moxon
   Declares there is nothing to pay
For the splendid attire
Which all must admire,
   Of the Church and State vollum – hoor-ray!
      Hoor – ray!
         Nothing to pay!!
   For the Church and State vollum in costly array.

My joy to complete
That book of 'the *Sweet*'
   'The Fall' – you remember the rest;
Enriched with his fine
Paw-writing divine
   Has flown home from the Stutfield nest.
    Flown from the nest
      Where 'twas caressed –
Long may the author be happy and blest.

[From a letter to Derwent Coleridge, 22 January 1852]

By the bye, talk of picters, how dar'd you come and hike away my
Poole picter of Father, and settle wi' Moxon, that it was to be the
frontispiece, without saying a word to poor I – good, bad or indif-
ferent? That's the way a poor drudge of a painstaking slave of a
co-editor is to be served by her '*elder brother*'. 'I'm your elder
brother, Miss!'

     Darran was a bold man
       And Darran was a bad –
     Darran came to my house
       And stole away my Dad.

     I'll go to Darran's house
       When Darran i'nt at home –
     Poke about his library
       To find his biggest tome.

Back I'll go to Darran's house
When Darran is in bed,
Seize upon his biggest tome,
And beat about his head.

To be serious, I know not how Allston's picture will engrave.

Doggrel Charm

To a little lump of malignity, on being medically assured that it was not a fresh growth, but an old growth splitting.

1

Split away, split away, split away, split!
Plague of my life, delay pretermit!
Rapidly, rapidly, rapidly go!
Haste ye to mitigate trouble and woe!

2

Then if you come again, done be His will
Who ordereth all things beyond human skill!
Patience he findeth who seeketh that need
Grace from the fountainhead comes at full speed.

3

Crack away, tumour, I pray thee to crack,
Just now you seem to be on the right track
But if you're in the wrong, right let me be,
And promptly submitting to Heaven's decree.

March 29th 1852

APPENDIX: 'HOWITHORN'

In her diary for 12 August 1848 SC referred to 'my little ballady metrical tale "The Way under the Lake". That poem was begun in the spring of the year before I undertook the article on B and F, which I finished at Margate in June – adding a few finishing strokes on my return home.' SC's review of the two editions of Beaumont and Fletcher by Alexander Dyce and George Darley was published in the *Quarterly Review* in September 1848 (see pp. 242–3, below), and it seems likely that once the article was finished she took up the tale again, with the new title 'Howithorn'. Two pages of the draft scheme of 'Howithorn' are dated 20 and 24 September 1848, and some of the rough outlines of verses are on the verso of pages in which she discusses Beaumont and Fletcher. Much of the story takes place by a lake and it includes a grand subterranean procession, so it seems almost certain that this is the same poem – I have found no traces of any other 'ballady metrical tales' in her papers. She also thought of entitling it 'Palfrey'.

Neither of SC's biographers mentions 'Howithorn', but there are 78 unnumbered pages of outlines, drafts and fragments in the HRC, so (despite her characteristically deprecating it as 'little') it was a major poetic undertaking, the longest poem in prospect of any she wrote. Some of the sketched material incorporates two of the poems of the 1840s 'written for *Phantasmion*', according to the Red Book – 'Ere I knew thee' (SC's slip, I assume, for 'Ere I loved thee') and 'The Melancholy Prince', p. 180 and p. 183 in this edition. That they seemed to SC transferable from *Phantasmion* to 'Howithorn' suggests the kinship between the two works, and moreover points to an important element of continuity in her creative life. She did not finish 'Howithorn', but she was most probably referring to it in a poignant letter dated 7 November 1851 and written to her brother Derwent during her mortal illness: 'I began a wild poem once. I sometimes wish I had not been diverted from it, and spent so much time on theology, which I was partly led to by my friend, de Vere'.

The poem is certainly wild. The setting seems at first to be the 'north countrie' of the Lake District, but it is also a magical world of witches and warriors, love and desertion, madness and disguise. The planned climax of the story takes place around a lake and an underground passage beneath it. Mainly written in six-line stanzas of three octosyllabic couplets, the poem has a freedom, boldness and narrative fluency reminiscent of the prose in *Phantasmion*.

Much of the manuscript material is indecipherable, fragmentary and provisional, but enough remains to give a sense of the kind of story SC was writing, and reasonably extended extracts of the verse. But a word of warning: although the text below is as accurate as I could make it, it includes gaps and conjectures, and some of the readings are dubious. I hope that the merit of some of the verses and the interest of seeing what SC was working on compensate for the less than ideally stable text.

The ten pages of MS notes outlining the story and certain scenes are not consecutive and are only partly decipherable; moreover, they were written at different times, and they are not entirely consistent internally (some of the names change, for instance); but they allow a reconstruction of a great deal of the story. For readers who are interested in recovering as far as possible the course of the narrative, I have included transcripts of relevant passages in the Notes on the Poems (pp. 242–5); but there are many dubious readings and hiatuses. For other readers, a brief plot synopsis follows, with caveats as to its reliability.

After a prologue about the unhappy marriage of 'Rufrabare and Thorniside', we discover that in their earlier life (or possibly in a parallel world) they were called Altamire and Howithorn. The young noble Altamire is betrothed to Likanare, the wealthy daughter of Godamoor. But Likanare before the marriage goes on a trip to see some of her kinsmen, including Howithorn and her brother Charelio. There she falls in love with Charelio and discovers that she never truly loved Altamire. Likanare runs away in male disguise as a warrior, intending to fight in battle alongside Charelio. He meanwhile has also fallen in love with her, and pursues her, crossdressing in his turn by adopting female disguise, in order to hide from his enemies in the regions where he is travelling. Likanare is taken into captivity by a witch and required by her to dissimulate her love and to feign madness. The abandoned Altamire (who is also, later in the story, to disguise himself, in his case as an old man) encounters Howithorn consoling Likanare's father. Partly to spite his father Cedreth, Altamire marries Howithorn, and they set off in quest of Likanare and Charelio.

The extracts I have managed to recover end about here, but the story continues towards a meeting of the protagonists near the lake. Howithorn falls into its transforming waters, and loses her memory and her sense of who she is. Various escapes, rescues and pursuits take place around the water and the subterranean passages beneath it. Eventually Charelio is to marry Likanare, and the quarreling married couple Altamire and Howithorn find that they actually love each other. These reconciliations take place amid a war between Cedreth and Clorian, the fathers respectively of Altamire, and of Charelio and Howithorn: the war is resolved by the marital harmony at the end. There is a subplot in which Altamire's aunt, Almantha (Themilda and Theaura in some drafts), falls in love with Charelio, but eventually she renounces her love and finally dies.

I have included six passages here, the last of these the most extended. They are prefaced with brief editorial indications of the situation in the narrative.

1. This seems to be a prologue to the poem, or possibly a first version before the story changed direction.

Rufrabare and Thorniside

There once was a pair in the North countrie
As oddly matched as a pair could be
The wife was a haughty handsome scold
Her partner longed that her days were told
She thought her spouse a tedious bore
And warmly wished that his days were o'er.

This pair a homestead chose to take
By the side of a dusky winding lake:
The husband's heart you might behold
In the leaden waters dark and cold:
His spouse's temper, sharp and hard,
In the rocks which stood the lake to guard.

Unto this lake doth a tale belong
As strange as ever was formed in song...

2. These stanzas recounting Altamire's betrothal to Likanare are headed 'Part 2. 1'.

The time had been when Rufrabare
Was gallant gay and debonair
His parents called him Altamire
And bade him high estate aspire
The nephew he of a maiden queen
Of lofty parts and noble mien

And courage high, might claim the hand
Of the richest fair in all the land;
[?These led for him] by an eager heart
He played with zeal the lover's part
To Likanare a gentle maid
Whose clear grey eye long lashes shade.

Still darker than her glowing tresses
Those soft and wavy wildernesses
That starred all o'er with jewels bright
Shewed like a balmy summer's night
Shadowing a tender moonlight scene
Her count'nance lucid and serene.

Fair was her eyebrow's jetty streak
The rose glowed faintly through her cheek
And yet it seemed to flourish too –
No lily shrined in morning dew
Or floating on the crystal water
Looked fresher than the graceful daughter

Of Godamoor who oft with pleasure
Gazed upon his living treasure
And thought when he should low be laid
His wealth should go to the lovely maid –
Meantime had giv'n her a noble dower
May line with gold her wedding bower.

Unless through many a mad vagary
Misled by fancies fond and airy
She cast away her charms divine
Like pearls before the [?rending] swine –
But little of such doom dreamèd she
Careless of gold and fancy free.

When Altamire his suit proposed
The bride with his rich offer closed:
The maid with no presentiment
Of change did to his wish consent
And deemed the youth with [?knighthood] fired
Was loved when he was but admired.

The marriage was a settled thing
To [?gladden] the last days of Spring
She smiled with no presentiment
Of change to come but gave consent
Before the passion was forsaken
The marriage vows were to be taken.

Meantime the maiden somewhat loth
When she had plighted forth a troth
A long vowed visit went to pay
To find a [?kinsman] far away...

3. Stanzas headed 'Part 2. 2 3.' Likanare falls in love with Howithorn's brother, Charelio.

The place whereto with palfrey fleet
And travelling equipage complete
The pensive placid fair was borne
Lay near the home of Howithorn,
And Howithorn's half-worshipped brother
The image of his angel mother:

Who, full of light and full of love
Yet brighter shone in heaven above
And he all loveliness and light
Than Howithorn more nobly bright
Ev'n here her latest mien displayed
[?Alone] for the betrothed maid.

That heart she thought her own no more
Till now had ne'er been given before
Till now had never strayed from home
At last too late it learns to roam
To love, for her, is but to grieve...

4. Likanare dreads the prospect of marriage to Altamire.

As one who, waked with sudden shock
Beholds o'erhead the falling rock
Thus Likanare, awake too late
With horror views impending fate;
And feels as one constrained to leap
Into the dim and smothering deep.

Those marriage bonds, that lately seemed,
When fruit of wedded love she dreamed,
Soft thornless wreaths with roses twined
Are now sharp swords with chains combined
Chains to enclose – a sword to sever
Her bleeding heart from joy for ever.

She dreams that tightest cords are wound
Her galled and shuddering hands around
That thus she's bound in the embrace
Of a stone statue face to face
Till she and it are one form grown
And she too slowly turns to stone.

5. In mental turmoil Likanare disguises herself as a warrior in armour.

One day it seemed her brain's confusion
Is shaping forth a new delusion.
She dwells on fights and fatal arms
On battle fierce and war's alarms
Resolves to seek the distant land
Where bold Charelio's legions stand:

To bear his arms whate'er betide
To fight and perish by his side
His helpmate bold if not his bride.
Next morn the maid was vainly sought
Charelio seeks as one distraught;

An armed youth at earliest dawn
He passed some shepherds in the lawn –
A slender form of middling height
In polished armour glittering bright
An aged woman by his side
Intent his hasty steps to guide:

Twas she twas she Charelio cries
And swifter than the falcon flies
A dove to seize he hastens on
The youth and mantle both are gone
Where do they roam that loveliest pair
Sad thought reechoes where ah where?

But how shall modest Likanare
The warrior man's armour wear
How came just on that strange disguise?
How such a train of subtle lies?
O marvel of all potent love
That makes a serpent of the dove!

Instructed by a beating heart
The guileless maiden practised art
[??Right curses] on the web she spun
A new thing underneath the sun,
A maidenly and tempered madness
More like a soft bewildered sadness.

It seemed as in her sovereign light
Of Reason yet shone clear and bright
While that subservient mind that brings
The knowledge of external things
The house's mind was overthrown
A misreporting mirror grown

She talks as though she were in thrall
In some great warrior's armed hall
And blesses oft captivity
That keeps her from worse durance free
Able to muse from morn to night
On one lov'd visage softly bright.

Wildly she sings then falls a weeping
And wanders forth at th'hour of sleeping
Sure love concealed has turned her brain
Now madness tears that veil in twain
Not May a [?warmer] sunshine beamed
When clearer than noonday it seemed

As waters in still nights of June
Shine quiet to the quiet moon
With calm bright smile Charelio viewed
The maid serene in tranquil mood
Gazed calmly at that tranquil beauty
Nor heaved a sigh at war with duty.

[…]
And now he feels a livelier passion
Love kindling up and admiration…

6. *Altamire, dejected at the loss of Likanare, bemoans his state, and then encounters Howithorn in the forest comforting Likanare's father. Stanzas headed 'Part 2 2'. SC has written 'Ere I knew thee' after the first stanza below, and 'The melancholy Prince' after the stanza ending 'He thus portrays his sad estate': I have taken these as instructions to interpolate the Red Books on pages 180 and 183, above.*

Meantime her lover left behind
Mused on her charms with constant mind
'My sky is dark, all dark,' he cries
'When will the Queen of Heav'n arise?
How long she tarries – Ah! how long!'
Then breathes his soul in ardent song.

1

Ere I loved thee what hue did the May blossoms wear,
And how were the rose and the woodbine attired:
When the notes of the nightingale floated in air,
Did I list to the music as if 'twere inspired? –
I ask not blest Lover – nor seek to recall
That season of dimness and winterly cold;
The sun is now shining – it shines over all,
And all things are painted with purple and gold.

Were the sun of my love blotted out from the sky,
How then would the rose and the woodbine appear?
When the lark sang his song as he mounted on high,
How then would his melody sound in mine ear? –
Full surely I know not: my seasons would fail,
Could I truly depicture that blackness and gloom:
Ere it comes may this joy-illumed cheek have grown pale,
And dark with the shadows that fall from the tomb.

The flowers of Spring are overblown
And Altamire's bright hopes are flown
Forsaken while the primrose dies
He on a couch of sickness lies
And all the glowing summer's bloom
Seems but to mock his helpless doom.

The rose her brightest line displays
When August on his spirit preys
The sun through radiant sapphire shines,
In him the light of life declines –
And careless of his future fate
He thus portrays his sad estate.

I see the sun rise while the shadows are waning,
But darkness alone in my spirit is reigning;
The Rivers are glad once again to be clad
In the rich golden light that he scatters around,
And with voices of pleasure the forests resound –
Ah! why do these visages, hideous and black,
Still frown upon me tho' the sun is come back?

The waters of Pleasure beside me are sweeping,
As fast as they flow all as fast am I weeping;
No drop do I taste while my hours run to waste,
For to me they are bitter as tears that I shed
And alas! it were fitter to lay down my head,
And to sink in the Earth, like the soft summer rain,
Than to gaze on the waters of Pleasure in vain.

I roam in the glades of the Forest alone:
The trees of my garden unlovely are grown:
But far as I range I can meet with no change;
A mist from within comes to darken my sight,
And rests on the landscape like fog or a blight –
Wan, frigid and cheerless all nature is seen,
Like hoar-frosted meadows despoiled of their green.

I envy the beasts that are seeking their prey,
And the vile slimy reptile that crawls in my way;
Yon carolling bird makes his joy to be heard –
Ah! now he is falling! – he carols no more! –
His shouting and singing and soaring are o'er! –
Yet I envy him still, as he falls on his nest,
With the sharp-pointed arrow stuck deep in his breast.

At length despair to anger yields
He dreams of war and bloody fields –
His Sire refusing war to wage
Swells beyond bounds his tide of rage
By high royal resentment torn
He first encounters Howithorn.

She came with fear and sorrow wild
To seek her mother's angel child –
And found the Sire of Likanare
Weeping her loss in deep despair
His woe her rising wrath represt
And soft compassion ruled her breast.

Within his old ancestral wood
Beneath an ancient oak she stood
There o'er the ancient man she bent
On consolation's work intent
Her golden locks around her streaming
Her eyes through crystal teardrops gleaming

Forth rushing in impetuous mood
By cares he fain would fly pursued
Sad Altamire overheard the fair
The tale of both their woes declare
The twain deceived, forsaken, slighted
In sorrows found – were fast united

Nay more mid all this inward strife
The youth sought Howithorn to wife.
His Sire and hers had long been foes
In days of yore their feud arose
And now it pleased him to be mated
With one whose house his father hated.

That father who with soul unkind
Had thus opposed his vengeful mind
The maiden [?light] behind his vows
Now took [him] for her lord and spouse
Still on her lost Charelio dreaming
Still to regain her treasure scheming

For oft he swore with zeal profound
To seek that youth the world around
Forsworn his hate and jealousy
Thus they in evil hour agree
The ties they formed to ease their pains
For now they find the heaviest chains.

Through many a land in search they went
But nowhere found their souls' content –
By storms within and storms without
For many a moon are cast about
In all their strong endeavours crossed
Like wandering vessels tempest-tossed.

At length, as when with sudden shock
A pinnace founders on a rock
Thus driven by the tyrant gale
They founder in the darksome vale
Till wrecked upon its dismal shore
All they have lost and gained deplore.

Said Altamire 'No more we'll roam
Here in the vale we'll fix our home
This vale so drear and desolate
The image of our mind and fate
I'll roam no more my heart is weary
Here leave we ne'er these mountains dreary'.

The visions of the past had faded
Their minds by darkening thoughts invaded
With disappointment she was vexed
And he with strangest thoughts perplexed.
Pale mists amid the mountains cast
Seemed spectres of their pleasures past.

'Oh not for love', thought she, 'but hate
And scorn he sought me for his mate'.
He never loved the poor forsaken
Not for my sake this hand was taken
How could I deem her bright and fair
Such such the lightning's lurid glare.

Thus musing on a bleak hill's side
Mid waves of mist the youth espied
Advancing forth a haggard form
That seemed the genius of the storm:
Far off turns like a mountain [?ash]
But close at hand a scanty [?bush].

A keen eyed crone, whose laughter shrill
Awaked the echoes of the hill,
Exclaimed – 'Charelio – I'll be sworn
No brother he of Howithorn:
Her Sire was wedded to his mother
Only in name is he her brother.

A well-framed tale, good easy youth
Has passed with you for simple truth
List to my counsel if you care
Yet to regain lost Likanare
And bound no more by hateful vows
Leave an unloved unloving spouse'.

Tempter avaunt! – he fiercely cried
No tempter I the witch replied
No counsellor of sin and shame
You might be free with none to blame
Not she herself proud Howithorn
But since your answer is her scorn

Fare well – The word was scarcely uttered
When thunder that but lately muttered
Now roars aloud – It seemed a spell
Depended on that word Farewell
So threatening grew the skiey crashes
So fiercely glare the lightning flashes

Alarmed by wind and flooding rain
The youth descends before the plain
That night upon his restless bed
He ponders all the beldame said
And on the morrow seeks the crag
Where late he saw the siren-hag.

But ere his steps that point attain
Loudly begins the hurricane
Shelter he seeks beneath a rock
Beside th' affrighted mountain flock
And seats himself in a mossy cave
Where safe he hears the tempest rave.

Here as he casts his eye around
He spies a letter on the ground
And writ thereon – 'To Altamire'
From one who reads his heart's desire;
Some little time he spends perusing
A longer space in anxious musing

Then suddenly upstarted he
As though he'd been stung by a wasp or a bee,
And home he went with a hurried pace
And entered his house with an altered face
And looked about for Thorniside
As a man might seek a darling bride…

Notes on the Poems

Except where these are clearly indicated in the title of the poem itself, I give the dates and provenance of each poem in the notes. Poems in the Red Book are described as '(RB)' after the title; poems from the five volumes of Children's Verses as '(CV1, CV3)', etc.; and poems only in manuscript as '(MS)'. For a list of other abbreviations used in the notes, see pp. 17–18.

When a poem has been previously published, I note the date and place of publication. With the exception of poems so indicated, all poems are published here for the first time. I have as far as possible dated the hitherto unpublished poems by year of composition. In many cases the date has been given on the manuscript itself, by SC or occasionally by other hands: these are dated in roman type. Some poems can be reliably dated by external evidence: these are dated in italic. For some the date of composition remains conjectural: these are dated in italic by year, with one or two question marks according to the extent of the evidence. For a few poems a range of possible dates has been given. I have given 1834 as the date of all the poems in the books of Children's Verses, but many of them were probably first written on SC's 'Herby cards' between 1831 and 1833, and then copied into the books in 1834.

I have in almost all cases attempted to give a chronological ordering of the poems. The main exception to this rule has been for the poems of 1843 in the Red Book (pp. 156–86), for which I have preferred to follow SC's own sequence in the Red Book instead of re-arranging them in strict chronology. The other exceptions are 'January brings the blast' (pp. 82–5) and 'Tennyson's "Lotos Eaters" with a new conclusion' (pp. 171-2), where I have departed from chronology in order to keep linked poems together as a group. The notes record the dates of composition as given in the Red Book.

Sara Coleridge's own notes to the poems in the Red Book are placed in quotation marks followed by (SC). I have given sources for allusions only where SC has signalled the allusion by using quotation marks. SC gives marginal alternatives for phrases, lines or stanzas in many of the poems. I have not made these alternatives part of the copy-text except when the corresponding lines of the main text have been deleted. This is not a variorum edition, but I have included the larger and more interesting variants in the notes. (See 'A Note on the Text', above, pp. 15–16).

Early Poems 1815-1829

Page 25. 'Valentine written in girlhood – perhaps at 13 years of age' (RB). 'A very youthful production' (SC). Line 31: Clytie – a water-nymph in love with Apollo; when her love was not returned, she stared fixedly at the sun. Line 35: Iphis – he killed himself for love of Anaxerete, whom the gods turned to stone to punish her for her hard-heartedness.

Hartley Coleridge's 'Valentine. To a fair Artiste. Written in 1813' may be a precedent for SC's inclusion of this poem in the Red Book. HC's poem is prefaced by a note: 'These, if not the first verses that I ever wrote, are the first with which I succeeded in pleasing even myself: – in fact, the first in which I was able to express a preconceived thought in metre' (*Poems*, ed. Derwent Coleridge (2 vols, 1851), ii. 145–6).

Page 26. 'Translated from Horace in early youth' (RB, 1815). From Horace's Ode, 1.5, 'Quis multa gracilis te puer in rosa'.

Page 27. 'Praises of a Country Life' (MS, 1817). The MS breaks off as shown. Compare the start of Pope's 'Ode on Solitude', another youthful effort, written, so Pope claimed, when he was not yet twelve years old: 'How happy he, who free from care / The rage of courts, and noise of towns; / Contented breathes his native air, / In his own grounds'.

Pages 25–59. The following 33 poems, with the exception of the 'Valentine to Rose Lynn', are all written in the Red Book in HNC's hand, his transcripts of Sara's poems up until their marriage in September 1829. He has dated each poem, and arranged them in chronological order, with the exception of the two earliest of these poems, the Petrarch translations from 1818 (pp. 29-30), which HNC has placed in the Red Book after 'To Edith May Southey…' from 1825 (p. 33). Many of the verses were originally included in SC's letters to HNC during their long engagement: this correspondence was destroyed by their children after SC's death.

Page 29. 'I dolci colli, ov'io lasciai me stesso' (RB, 1818). From Petrarch's sonnet 209 in the *Canzoniere*; the first line could be translated as 'The gentle hills where I left my being'.

Page 30. 'Vago augelletto, che cantando vai' (RB, 1818). From Petrarch's sonnet 353; the first line could be translated as 'Stray little bird, you wander round singing'.

Page 30. 'Extract from an Epistle from Emma to Henry' (RB, Summer 1823).

Page 32. 'To Elizabeth S. K. Poole' (RB, May 27 1823).

Page 32. 'To Zoe King' (RB, 1823). SC's first Commonplace Book includes a matching poem of twelve lines from Zoe, dated 5 June 1823, beginning 'With wonder and delight I hail / Thee, lovely Lily of the Vale'.

Page 33. 'To Edith May Southey during absence on the Lily of the Nile'

(RB, 1825). SC named her daughter after Edith Southey, her cousin and childhood companion.

Page 34. '[Valentine to Rose Lynn]' (MS, 1826). Below the poem there is a note in an unknown hand: 'From Sara Coleridge to Rose C. Lynn. Feb. 1826. Keswick'. Rose Lynn was the daughter of James Lynn, the rector of Keswick.

Page 34. 'My dear dear Henry!' (RB, 1827). Line 1: 'Wad some Power the giftie gie you' – Robert Burns, 'To a Louse', lines 43-4: 'O wad some Pow'r the giftie gie us / *To see oursels as others see us!*'.

Page 35. 'To the tune of "When icicles hang by the wall"' (RB, 1827). 'When icicles hang by the wall' is Winter's song at the end of *Love's Labour's Lost*, V.ii.895-912. Line 12: '"To dispossess the present hour"' – from Matilda Betham, *The Lay of Marie* (1816), Canto 1: 'Restless awaits the Minstrel's power / To dispossess the present hour'.

Page 35. 'Sequel' (RB, 1827).

Page 36. 'Let it not a Lover pique' (RB, 1827).

Page 36. 'How now, dear suspicious Lover!' (RB, 1827).

Page 37. 'Now to bed will I fly,' (RB, 1827). 'This doggrel, to transcribe which was a lover-like proceeding indeed, was written from the Grove Highgate, I think in the autumn of 1826. I had suffered sadly in London from these night tormentors' (SC). HNC gives 1827 as the date.

Page 38. 'They tell me that my eye is dim, my cheek is lily pale,' (RB, 1827).

Page 39. 'Go, you may call it madness, folly – &c.' (RB, 1827, and MS, 1904). Parodying Samuel Rogers, 'To ———': 'Go! you may call it madness, folly; / You shall not chase my gloom away! / There's such a charm in melancholy / I would not if I could be gay'. A further MS of the poem in EC's hand, dated 14 December 1904, is headed 'Parody of Rogers. Written by Sara Coleridge, when practising economy, with a view to "marrying a poor man" ... Contained in a letter of about 1827, to HNC, two years before their marriage. The whole correspondence was destroyed by their son and daughter, in the winter of 1853, as being too "sacred" to be left to fall into any other hands.'

Page 39. 'O! once again good night!' (RB, 1827).

Page 40. 'Art thou too at this hour awake,' (RB, 1827).

Page 41. 'To Louisa and Emma Powles' (RB, 1827). Line 23: Urganda – an enchantress, the wife of Alquif.

Page 42. 'Yes! With fond eye my Henry will peruse' (RB, 1827).

Page 43. '"How swift is a thought of the mind"' (RB, 1828). Line 3: 'Three hundred long miles', the distance between SC in Keswick and HNC in London.

Page 44. 'Verses to my Beloved with an empty purse' (RB, 1828).

Page 47. 'My Henry, like a modest youth,' (RB, 1828).

Page 48. 'To Mrs Whitbread' (RB, 1828).

Page 49. 'O, how, Love, must I fill' (RB, 1828).

Page 50. 'When this you see' (RB, 1828).

Page 50. '"I am wreathing a garland for wintry hours",' (RB, 1828).

Page 51. 'Henry comes! No sweeter music' (RB, 1828).

Page 52. 'To Susan Patteson with a purse' (RB, 1828).

Page 53. 'Th'enamour'd Nymph, whose faithful voice' (RB, 1828).

Page 53. 'Epistle from Sara to her sister Mary whom she has never yet seen, her "Yarrow Unvisited"' (RB, 1828, and MS, 27 April 1828); there is a third surviving copy of the poem, SC's most ambitious up to this point, in Mary's commonplace book: stanzas 1, 6, 13, 14, and 16 of this third text appear in Hainton, p. 112, and include a few very minor variants.

The poem is addressed to Mary Pridham, who was engaged to Sara's brother Derwent; she went on to become one of SC's closest confidantes and friends, and the recipient of several hundred of her letters. SC's was not her first Coleridge family verse greeting: STC had sent her a poem in a letter dated 16 October 1827: 'Dear tho' unseen! Tho' I have left behind / Life's gayer views and all that stir the mind, / Now I revive, Hope making a new Start... / A Father's blessings on thee, gentle Maid!' (Hainton, p. 110, *STCL* vi. 705). Completing the family's poetic greetings, rather late in the day, Hartley wrote Mary *his* epistolary poem in August 1830, beginning 'Mary, our eyes are strangers, but our hearts / Are strongly knitted in strong bonds of love / For one, whom love of thee hath sanctified' ('To my unknown Sister in Law', in *Poems*, 1851, i. 114–16).

In Wordsworth's 'Yarrow Unvisited', published in 1807, the poet prefers not to endanger his imagined vision of Yarrow by actually going there: in SC's 'Scale of WW's poetry', the poem is ranked at 'a a a', her second highest rating (*EC*, p. 267).

In the 27 April 1828 MS, SC has put two phrases in quotation marks: line 75: 'thoughtless follies' – from Burns, 'A Bard's Epitaph', line 23; and 'soiling earth', from Wordsworth, 'To HC Six years old', line 29. In this MS she also supplies a note to 'the elm-tree's lace-like vest' in line 82: 'STC pointed out to me the lacelike appearance of the elm's foliage' (SC).

Lines 45–8: 'to safe dry land / His sylph-like sister oft he bore' – oft but not always – see 'The Plunge' (above, p. 102, and below, p. 221). The phrase '"sylph-like Sister"' is in quotation marks in Mary's commonplace book; the young Sara was delicate and diminutive, and would often find herself compared to a fairy or sylph. Dorothy Wordsworth, for instance, spoke of her as 'a little Fairy! A spirit! A thing that hardly seems to touch the earth as she skims along' (letter to Lady Beaumont, 25 July 1804, *DWL*, p. 405), and her brother Hartley remembered her as a girl in similar terms: 'perfectly a Fairy, a being belonging neither to time or space, so like the etherial vehicle of a pure spirit, a visible soul (I remember once when she was sitting at the

Piano-forte at Greta Hall she told me I was a *visible fool* for saying so) that I cannot image any thing like her' (HCL, p. 156). When she came to London in 1822, she was hailed as 'exquisite Sara', 'flower of the lakes' and 'sylph of Ullswater' (Griggs, p. 39). Lines 86–8: 'the tropic land' – HNC's poor health had led to his trip to the West Indies in late 1824, which he wrote up in his book *Six Months in the West Indies in 1825* (1826). Lines 95–100: 'my brother's wayward fate' – in Derwent's last years at Cambridge he had run up debts, neglected his studies, and for a brief period lost his religious faith (Hainton, pp. 29–45). Lines 149–52: 'these visions of my own' – alluding to 'Yarrow Unvisited': 'We have a vision of our own; / Ah! why should we undo it?' (lines 51–2). SC draws a conclusion at odds with Wordsworth's.

Page 58. 'The Rose of Love my Henry sends,' (RB, 1828). HNC has recorded variant phrasings for line 14 – 'And cultured by a blissful pair' – and line 16 – 'And shed thy sweetest fragrance there!'

Page 58. ''Mid blooming fields I daily rove'' (RB, 1829). SC and HNC were married on 3 September 1829, which for Sara meant moving from the Lake District to begin life in London. Lines 31–2: 'To dwell 'mid smoke and pent up nooks' – compare STC, 'Frost at Midnight', 'I was reared / In the great city, pent 'mid cloisters dim' (lines 52–3).

Page 59. 'Those parched lips I'd rather press' (RB, 1829). This is the last of SC's poems transcribed by HNC into the Red Book. The next time he takes the book up is for nine pages of materials by and about STC, a month before the latter's death in July 1834. He makes notes of STC's conversation on 28 June and 5 July, transcribes his 'Letter to a Godchild' of 13 July (later included in the 1849 edition of *Confessions of an Inquiring Spirit*), records STC's death on 25 July, and makes notes towards the biographical records of his life.

Poems 1829–1843

Page 60. 'Sickness' (RB, 1832). 'Written during my long illness after the birth of Edith in 1832' (SC). Edith Coleridge was born on 2 July 1832. SC's dialogue-essay on 'Nervousness', written in 1834, tries to come to terms with her illness (Mudge, pp. 201–16). Line 14: 'faultering' is SC's spelling.

Page 61. 'Written in my Illness at Hampstead during Edith's Infancy' (RB, 1832 or 1833). Line 6: '"fever of the languid heart"' – Wordsworth, 'The Female Vagrant', 'Fretting the fever round the languid heart' (line 206).

Page 62. 'Verses written in sickness 1833, before the Birth of Berkeley and Florence' (RB, 1833, and MS written by Mrs STC). 'Sara Coleridge to her Husband, Mother, and Children. Written on my Mother's bed, November 7th 1833, Hampstead' (SC). Alongside the title SC has written 'By SC, copied out by her dear mother', and above the poem she has transcribed her mother's description of it as 'An affecting poem composed by my dear Sara during sickness a few weeks previous to the Birth of her twin infants, Berkeley and Florence'. The twins Berkeley and Florence Coleridge were born in January 1834, but survived only a few days. There is also an MS of the poem in Mrs STC's handwriting, in an envelope on which SC has written 'Verses by Sara Coleridge in Nervous Illness before the Birth of the Twins'. It seems likely that SC transcribed her mother's copy of the poem into the Red Book, including some minor revisions.

Pages 63-110. The next 57 poems are all either taken (or, in two cases, adapted) from SC's five volumes of Children's Verses and *Pretty Lessons in Verse for Good Children*. I have dated all as 1834, but some of them will have been written earlier, before being copied from the 'Herby cards' into the bound volumes. Herbert was born in 1830, and Edith in 1832.

Page 63. 'To Herbert Coleridge. Feb 13 1834' (CV1). Written on the inside cover of the first of SC's MS books of children's verses.

Pages 64-79. These eighteen poems were all published in *PL*. All are copied from CV1 except for 'Foolish Interference' (page 67), from CV2.

Page 64. 'Benoni. Dedication' (*PL* and CV1). Title: 'Benoni' – Benjamin, the son of Jacob and Rachel, was called 'Benoni' by his dying mother. The word is Hebrew for 'son of my sorrow'.

Page 65. 'The Months' (*PL* and CV1). This became a well-known nursery song: Edmund Blunden recalled hearing it sung to him when he was a child. It has been published three times as a children's book, illustrated by Jenni Oliver, Normand Chartier and Elizabeth Falconer. In the 1950s Flanders and Swann did a grumbly parody, 'A Song of the Weather', as I learned from Kevin Jackson: 'January brings the snow / Makes your feet and fingers glow. / February's ice and sleet / Freeze the toes right off your feet', and so on.

Page 66. 'The Nightingale' (*PL* and CV1). Lines 7-9: 'some aver, no need hath she / The voice of grief to borrow. // No, 'tis the merry Nightingale' – among the averrers was STC in 'The Nightingale', from the 1798 *Lyrical Ballads*.

Page 70. 'Poppies' (*PL* and CV1). SC wrote to Emily Trevenen in January 1835 that 'the Poppy poem in "Pretty Lessons" should have been left out – some other doggerel substituted – but I was poorly'. However, the poem remained in later editions of the book. Line 4: 'cramasie' – crimson.

Page 73. 'Edith Asleep' (*PL* and CV1). SC's account of the genesis of *Phantasmion*, the fairy-tale which she wrote in 1835–6, has a bearing on the dream-life she imagines here and in the next poem, 'The Blessing of Health':

> I should never have put together such a string of waking dreams, if I had
> not been confined to my couch indoors, withdrawn from those sights of

natural objects which I had been taking in, during my whole childhood and early youth, incessantly. As sailors in the calenture see bright green fields in the ocean, so I saw with a special sadness and delight those shows of mother-earth from which I was so wholly shut out, as to the outward eye. They rose before me clad with 'the light that never was on sea or land', but which I faintly – very faintly – portrayed.

(Draft of letter to Mr. Pridham, 18 September 1844).

The quoted phrase, to which SC often alludes, comes from Wordsworth's 'Elegiac Stanzas, suggested by a picture of Peele Castle' (line 15). See also 'The Blessing of Health', pp. 74–5, above.

Page 75. 'The Humming-Birds' (*PL* and CV1). Line 5: 'Collibree' – more often spelt 'colibri', another term for 'humming-bird'. Lines 61–2: 'Can tiniest birds such passions know? / Does fire in downy bosoms glow?' – probably remembering *The Rape of the Lock*, Canto 1, lines 11-12: 'In tasks so bold, can little Men engage, / And in soft Bosoms, dwells such mighty Rage?'

Page 78. 'Providence' (*PL* and CV1). 'Childish Tears' and 'Providence' are the final two poems in the English section of *Pretty Lessons* before the 'Lessons in Latin'.

Page 79. A small selection of two of the 26 poems and 40 pages of the 'Lessons in Latin' section of *PL*.

Page 80. 'The Celandine' (CV1). Compare Wordsworth's 'The Lesser Celandine'. Wordsworth's flower shrinks 'In close self-shelter, like a thing at rest' (line 8), but SC fancies it to be more generous.

Page 80. 'January is the first month in the year' (MS, *1834?*). Written on a single sheet folded to make a little four-sided booklet.

Page 82. 'January brings the blast' (MS, *1837?*, revising CV1). This MS revises 'January freezes fast', one of the months poems from CV1 (not included in this edition). The MS is Herbert's transcription of the poem, on which Sara has made extensive changes and deletions, making a new version suitable for an older child with a more developed vocabulary.

Page 85. 'Little Sister Edith now' (CV1a).

Page 86. 'Why those tears my little treasure' (CV1a). 'Not this' has been pencilled at the head of this poem, probably rejecting it as too dark when SC was considering contenders for a second book of children's verses.

Pages 87-105. The next 26 poems come from CV2, unless otherwise specified. The first nine poems, up to 'The Crag-fast sheep', are the first nine in CV2. The title poem of CV2, 'The Feline Family', not included here, is one of the longer poems in the volume, fifteen 8-line stanzas about predatory cats.

Page 87. 'Sara Coleridge for Herbert and Edith. April 19th 1834' (CV2).

This dedicatory poem is on the inside cover of CV2, the counterpart of 'To Herbert Coleridge. Feb 13 1834' in the same position in CV1.

Page 87. 'Eye has not seen nor can the heart of man conceive the blessedness of Heaven' (CV2). The title is from 1 Corinthians 2:9: 'But as it is written, Eye hath not seen, nor ear heard, neither have entered into the heart of man, the things which God hath prepared for them that love him', alluding to Isaiah 64:4: 'For since the beginning of the world men have not heard, nor perceived by the ear, neither hath the eye seen, O God, beside thee, what he hath prepared for him that waiteth for him.'

Page 88. 'Consolation in Trouble' (CV2). Line 12: '"long themselves to go"' – source unknown.

Page 90. 'Grief's heavy hand hath swayed the lute;' (CV2). In a later hand SC has written 'Phantasmion' at the top of this poem. This earlier version of the poem can be compared to the secularised revision in *Phantasmion*, p, 123, above.

Page 91. 'The Little Invalid' (RB and CV2). In RB the poem is followed, unchronologically, by 'To My Son', another poem of advice to Herbert, written many years later, perhaps when he was going to university (see pp. 169-71 in this edition). Line 11: CV2 reads 'But then I have found that wherever they are'. Lines 21-24: in CV2 'Sweet Patience is ever by Charity's side, / Whom Jesus our blessed Redeemer loved well: / And she with strong Faith will our pilgrimage guide / Where He and his Holiest Comforter dwell'. Line 31: 'time ere it flies' – 'time as it flies' (CV2).

Page 94. 'Forget me not' (RB and CV2). In the Red Book SC has put this poem and the next, 'The Staining of the Rose', in a section called 'Flower Poems'. Other flower poems from CV2 – the purple columbine, water lily, and daffodil – are included in this edition, though not in the Red Book (see pp. 94, 99 and 105).

In CV2 the heroine is called 'Melene'.

Page 96. 'The Staining of the Rose' (RB and CV2). Lines 9-10 are in RB but not CV2.

Page 97. 'When Herbert's Mama was a slim little Maid' (MS, *1834*), published in Griggs, pp. 27–8. (Griggs divided it into eight-line stanzas, the MS being unclear as to stanza breaks; but the two source poems in CV2 each have stanzas of four lines.) The MS, a single sheet folded into four sides, is a gathering of three of SC's poems which she gave to her nephew Derwent Moultrie Coleridge, 'to make him laugh': the others are 'My Derwent! may you study Nature's book' and 'Fine birds and their plain wives'. 'Derwy's Papa is Br. Of Sara, Herbert's Mama, and Cousin of Edith', SC explains in a note.

There is a different and shorter version (without verses 4, 5 and 8) in CV2, with the title 'When Mama was young':

When Herbert's mama was a slim little maid

And lived among mountains and rivers and lakes,
With Derwent her brother she wandered and played,
And both of them gardened with spades and with rakes.

And godmama Edith was then a young girl,
Like any young kid she would gambol and dance:
In summer they loved in the meadows to whirl,
And over the rocks and the heather to prance.

A river ran close by the house where they dwelt;
A wood full of harebells was near to their home:
They bathed in the river – its coolness they felt,
And gathering wild-flowers did happily roam.

With Dora and Mary they went to the grove
And picked purple bilberries near the bright Lake:
They oft with each other in gathering strove;
An excellent pie did their bilberries make.

And oft they would gather the primroses pale,
And fill their nice baskets with sweet smelling flow'rs;
To make primrose wine and their friends to regale
Was one of their pleasures in Summer's gay hours.

In the poem sent to DMC, SC has combined the five verses of 'When
Mama was young' with verses 2-4 of 'Young days of Edith and Sara' (see
note to this poem, pp. 2210–1, below).

Page 98. 'Summer' (CV2). In CV2 this poem immediately follows the
much sunnier 'When Mama was young'.

Page 101. 'Written on a blank leaf of 'Naturalist's' Magazine' (MS, 1834).
'Naturalist's Magazine' – *The Naturalist's Library* (1833–45) by William
Jardine. SC wrote to Emily Trevenen on 27 April 1834 wishing she could
show her nephew Derwent 'Jardine's birds and monkeys as I do my own
chicks'. Line 11: 'with gentleness keeps pace' – from Wordsworth,
'Composed on the Eve of the Marriage of a Friend in Grasmere', lines 7-8:
'she, whose thoughts keep pace / With gentleness'. Lines 17-18 (under SC's
signature): 'May Derwent be studious learned and wise, / And delight in
the things of earth, water and skies' – SC rewrites for the next generation
some lines which STC had included in a letter of February 1807 to DMC's
father when he was a boy. STC's verses are mainly about poetic metre, with
near their conclusion the lines: 'If Derwent be innocent, steady, and wise,
/ And delight in the Things of Earth, Waters, and Skies; / Tender Warmth
at his Heart, with these metres to shew it, / With sound Sense in his Brains,
may make Derwent a Poet!' (*STCL*, iii.641)

Page 101. 'Young Days of Edith and Sara' (CV2). A companion piece to
'When Mama was young' (see above, pp. 219–20, note to 'When Herbert's

Mama was a slim little Maid'), as is shown by the fact that SC spliced together stanzas from each in the poem she sent to her nephew Derwent in 1834.

Page 102. 'The Plunge' (CV2). Compare the account of the same incident in SC's unfinished 'Autobiography', written in 1851:

> something happened to me, when I was two years old, which was so striking as to leave an indelible trace on my memory. I fancy I can even now recall, though it *may* be but the echo or reflection of past remembrances, my coming dripping up the Forge Field, after having fallen into the river behind the rails of the high wooden bridge that crossed the river Greta, which flowed behind the Greta Hall Hill. The maid had my baby cousin Edith, 16 months younger than I, in her arms; I was rushing away from Derwent, who was fond of playing the elder brother, on the strength of his two years' seniority, when he was trying in some way to control me, and, in my hurry, slipped from the bridge into the current. Luckily for me young Richardson was still at work in his father's forge. He doffed his coat and rescued me from the water. I had fallen from a considerable height, but the strong current of the Greta received me safely. I remember nothing of this adventure but the walk home through the field. I was put between blankets on my return to the house; but my constitution had received a shock, and I became tender and delicate, having before been a thriving child, & called by my Uncle Southey 'fat Sall' (Mudge, pp. 251–2).

Dorothy Wordsworth wrote about the accident, without reference to Derwent, in a letter to Lady Beaumont of 11 June 1805: 'We expect Mrs. C. at the end of this week – she is to bring the little Darling Sara with her, who has by the mercy of God escaped from an accident that you will shudder to hear of. She slipped from the Servant who was playing with her near the Forge at the bottom of the field, ran upon a wooden bridge, which I believe has been built since you were at Keswick, and fell into the Greta – the Bridge is very high above the Stream, and the water was low – it is almost miraculous that she was not dashed to pieces. A man from the forge went a considerable way down the river and took her out. She was put to bed immediately and soon recovered, but she has never been *perfectly* well since: Mrs. C. hopes however that change of air will entirely restore her' (*DWL*, p. 502).

Pages 106-110. The next six poems come from CV3.

Page 106. 'Fine birds and their plain wives' (CV3 and MS, 1834 – see note to 'When Herbert's Mama', p. 219). There is a further MS in the Coleridge collection at the Victoria University Library of Toronto University. Line 9: 'The gaudy bird of China' – 'The Ocellated Turkey with blue eyes in his tail and yellow bands' (SC).

Page 108. 'Herbert looking at the Moon' (CV3). In 'The Nightingale' STC described the infant Hartley looking at the moon:

> once, when he awoke
> In most distressful mood (some inward pain
> Had made up that strange thing, an infant's dream –)
> I hurried with him to our orchard-plot,
> And he beheld the moon, and, hushed at once,
> Suspends his sobs, and laughs most silently,
> While his fair eyes, that swam with undropped tears,
> Did glitter in the yellow moon-beam!   (lines 98–105)

Page 110. 'From Isles far over the Sea' (CV3). The different indentation and metrics within the poem are as shown in CV3.

Page 110. 'Seek first the Kingdom of Heaven' (RB, 1835?). 'These stanzas were written at Hampstead, I think before Phantasmion was begun. They are transcribed merely for curiosity, as a bit of the history of my mind. Oct 26 1851' (SC). According to her journal, SC wrote a first version of *Phantasmion* between October 1835 and January 1836.

Title: 'Seek first the Kingdom of Heaven' – 'But seek ye first the kingdom of God, and his righteousness; and all these things shall be added unto you', Matthew 6:33. Line 2: '"well attired"' – 'the well-attired woodbine', 'Lycidas', line 146.

Page 112. 'A Sister's Love' (MS *1836??*). This poem and 'From Petrarch' are written on a sheet of paper folded into four pages, without indication of date. The handwriting suggests a date in the second half of the 1830s, and 'clouds of nameless Sorrow' (line 2) could describe SC's intense depression and nervous collapse which came to a crisis in late 1836. 'Study's graver toil' and 'restless hopes of fame' (lines 7-9) suggest the concentrated theological study which she began in these years, and which contributed to her editorial work on STC. SC was deeply attached to her sister-in-law Mary, the addressee of 'Epistle from Sara to her sister Mary whom she has never yet seen...', pp. 53-7, above.

Page 113. 'From Petrarch' (MS, *1836??*). Written on the same sheet of paper as 'A Sister's Love', but much harder to decipher and almost illegible in parts. From the second paragraph onwards the poem is derived loosely and freely from canzone 126 in Petrarch's *Canzoniere* ('Chiare, fresche e dolci acque,'), particularly lines 40-65, although Petrarch's original does not use rhyming couplets. SC's interest in Petrarch spanned most of her life, from early translation exercises to her comment in a letter of 6 August 1850, on reading the recently published *In Memoriam*, that 'There is a very Italian air in this set of mourning poems throughout, as far as I have read. It is Petrarch come again, and become an Englishman' (to Aubrey de Vere, *EC*, p. 454).

Line 31: 'I [?sighed]' – the word is indecipherable and not really recognisable as 'sighed', which I supply nonetheless on the grounds of the corresponding line (61) in Petrarch: 'ch' i' dicea sospirando'.

Pages 114-40. The next thirty-five poems were published in *Phantasmion*. Although SC did not transcribe them into the Red Book, she did compile there a 'List of Poems in *Phantasmion*', giving first lines and page numbers. She also included a carefully handwritten 'Index to the Lyrics' in the copy she gave to Hartley; so there is some evidence she wished them to be seen beyond the context of the story.

Page 114. 'Tho' I be young – ah well-a-day!' The song is divided into two, with 'a pause in the soft strain' before the last two stanzas.

Page 116. 'Sylvan stag, securely play'. This poem and its two continuations ('Bound along or else be still' and 'Milk-white doe, 'tis but the breeze') are transcribed by SC from CV3, where they appear together as a single nine-stanza poem under the title 'On Buffon's remark that Spring is not a hunting season partly on account of the strong scent of the flowers'.

Page 117. 'Bound along or else be still'. In the poem in CV3 these two stanzas appear as the fifth and fourth respectively.

Page 117. 'Milk-white doe, 'tis but the breeze'. SC will have remembered the 'milk-white doe' in Wordsworth's *White Doe of Rylstone*, a favourite poem of her youth. In 1827 she had given HNC a quarto edition with her own extensive marginalia. She told HNC that she was grateful for the poem's real consolatory powers, and in a letter to Mrs Henry Jones she considered it 'to exhibit the power of faith in upholding the most anguish-stricken soul through the severest trials, and the ultimate triumph of the spirit, even while the frail mortal body is giving way' (*EC*, p. 111, letter of July 1835).

Page 123. 'Grief's heavy hand hath swayed the lute'. Compare the version of this song in CV2, p. 90, above.

Page 125. 'How gladsome is a child, and how perfect is his mirth'. SC returned to the setting of this song for the poem 'Children' in her Red Book, in which the final verse here figures as the sixth verse of eight. See pp. 185–6, above, and 237, below.

Page 134. 'Methought I wandered dimly on'. The song has a powerful effect: 'Gradually Melledine's voice, together with the fumes of the liquor which had been spilled upon the floor, infected the hearers with drowsiness, and, as the song proceeded, the scenes it pictured stole upon their misted eyes: first dim star-light, then Love with torch and lamp and beamy smile emerging from a wood, till at last a crowd of witching faces, and bright torches, and lamps of a thousand shapes and colours, lit and unlit, waved along before them in endless succession' (*Phantasmion*, p. 310).

Page 135. '"The spring returns, and balmy budding flow'rs'. There is a version of this poem in CV2, with the note 'Taken for *Phantasmion*'. It is entitled 'Return of Spring', and includes a number of minor variants, including 'my Herbert's' in line 6 instead of 'my darling's'.

Page 141. 'The Three Humpbacked Brothers' (RB, *1839??*). This is the sole poem of a section headed 'Juvenile Poems' in the Red Book. There is no indication of its date, but it seems to belong with some of the comic narratives from the middle to later 1830s in CV2 and CV3. SC notes at the head of the poem 'Recollections of one of the Tartarian Tales'. She was remembering 'The Story of the Little Hunchback', the seventh tale of *The Arabian Nights' Entertainments*.

Page 145. 'Reflections on Reading Lucretius' (MS, *1839??*). Parts of the poem are apparently in a final state, but it is not complete. The first nine stanzas are close to a fair copy, but the rest of the poem is in rougher draft, especially the final three stanzas.

SC reflects in particular on the famous passage in Lucretius about the sacrifice of Iphianassa (*De Rerum Natura*, 1.80–101). She also draws on a passage in which Lucretius praises the philosopher Epicurus for being undaunted by fables of the gods at a time when humanity was widely oppressed by religious beliefs (1.61–9). Lucretius relates how Iphianassa (thus in *Iliad* Book 9, but more often referred to as Iphigenia by later authors), sailing to Aulis in the expectation that she was to marry Achilles, was instead put to death by her father Agamemnon at the instigation of the priest Calchas. Calchas had said that this was necessary in order to appease the goddess Diana, and provide a following wind for the Greek fleet in its expedition to Troy.

SC thought *De Rerum Natura* 'one of the great poems of the world' and its opening address to Venus finer than anything in Dante (*EC*, pp. 291–5, 1846 letter to de Vere). When her cancer was diagnosed, she wrote in her diary: 'Oh! surely this deep spirit cannot have an end thus. We must live again. There must be truth in all that sages have believed. Lucretius could make up his mind to annihilation – Yet all the while what life – what activity expended on proving his miserable creed' (28 September 1850).

Line 69: 'Trivia's Aulic fane': the shrine in Aulis at the crossroads where three roads met (hence Tri-via), and the sacrifice took place. Line 97: 'Such bad religion flows from fear'. SC adapts Lucretius' famous line 'Tantum Religio potuit suadere malorum' ('Religion has been able to persuade men to do so many evil things') – a line she was also later to quote in her theological dialogues on 'Regeneration', in the context of what she considered the errors of Roman Catholicism.

Page 149. From 'Kings of England from the Conquest' (MS, *1840?*, excerpts published in Griggs). SC's little history goes from William the Conqueror to Queen Victoria. With the notable and unexplained exception of Elizabeth I, it includes queens as well as kings. The accession date of

1602 for James I is SC's slip: Elizabeth died on 24 March 1603.

Page 153. 'Receipt for a Cake' (MS, *1841??*). Undated MS laid into SC's second Commonplace Book, perhaps from the early 1840s. 'This was merely a Specimen for an intended rhyming Cookery Book thought of for a Bazaar, but never executed' (SC). Earlier in the album HC wrote a jocular poem 'I sing Minced Pie, the pride of Christmas cheer', so culinary rhyming had family precedent; HC's verses were published as 'Minced-Pie; A Christmas Carol. To Miss S——' in *Blackwood's Magazine* (February 1828), pp. 252–5.

Page 155. 'Lines on the Death of——' (MS, *1843?*). The poem is written on one of the cancelled sheets of SC's 'Regeneration' dialogues from 1850-51, but it is likely to be a reconstruction from memory of a lost poem she wrote on the death of HNC in 1843: SC's prefatory note to her poems in the Red Book records that she has no copy of some poems 'on my feelings about death after the loss of Henry'.

It is not clear quite how close the MS is to a fair copy. The MS suggests that the first and third stanza were intended to be inescapably circular; but they may perhaps be versions of one intended stanza. The second stanza has a different metric from the first and third, and SC has written 'gloom' in the margin, as if she was looking to continue the ABABBCBC scheme; but lines 13-14 here take a different rhyme. I have regularised the indentations of lines 5-8 and 13-14, all of which are indented in the MS. The minimal punctuation is as shown.

In a notebook labelled 'Deaths of Relations and Friends' SC recounts the final days of Henry's illness: 'Thursday Jan 26 [1843]. This day at 10 minutes to one o'clock my most beloved and honored husband breathed his last – James [Coleridge] and I sitting beside his bed. So ends the great charm of this world to me. H has made all things bright to me for 20 years – perhaps too bright. It is time to look at the brightness that can never fade.'

Poems 1843–1852

Page 156. 'For my Father on his lines called "Work Without Hope"' (RB, 1845, 'For A. de V.', and MS, no date), first published in full in Griggs, p. 166 (the first stanza had appeared in *EC*, p. 63). Mudge infers that the writer is 'presumably close to death' (p. 177), but the poem is clearly dated 1845 in RB, seven years before SC's death.

This is the first poem which SC transcribed in the Red Book, and it comes directly after nine pages of HNC's editorial notes on and extracts from STC; her 'Index to the following Poems' starts on the same page as HNC's final notes on STC's biography. There is a visible continuity, then, in this first poem being about her late father and her late husband. Her overall heading above this poem is 'Poems of Sara Coleridge in Widowhood'.

Line 1: 'amaranths' – the amaranth (or 'pigweed') was a fabled never-fading flower, emblem of poetic immortality. Line 13: 'whether Winter "slumbering, dreams of Spring"' – alluding to STC's 'Work Without Hope', lines 3-4. The whole poem reads as follows in the edition of his poems edited by SC and DC:

Work Without Hope
Lines Composed 21st February, 1827

All Nature seems at work. Slugs leave their lair –
The bees are stirring – birds are on the wing –
And Winter slumbering in the open air,
Wears on his smiling face a dream of Spring!
And I, the while, the sole unbusy thing,
Nor honey make, nor pair, nor build, nor sing.
 Yet well I ken the banks where amaranths blow,
Have traced the fount whence streams of nectar flow.
Bloom, O ye amaranths! Bloom for who ye may,
For me ye bloom not! Glide, rich streams, away!
With lips unbrighten'd, wreathless brow, I stroll:
And would you learn the spells that drowse my soul?
Work without hope draws nectar in a sieve,
And hope without an object cannot live.

In a letter of 25 February 1844 Hartley Coleridge wrote to SC: 'I am or should be very busy – but work without hope – you know the strain' (HRC).

At the end of the fair copy of the poem in RB, SC has redrafted the final stanza, with several possible alternatives for line 16 – 'While from her garland half the leaves are shed / From her full garland half the honours shed' – and a new line 18: 'Replace the roses on my drooping head. –'. The drafted stanza ends with alternative new versions of its last line: 'but backward cast / Mine eye still seeks <to find> the Future in the Past. / Fain would mine eye discern the Future in the Past.'

Another MS of the poem, not dated, also ends 'Fain would mine eye discern the Future in the past'.

Page 157. 'Friend, thou hast been a traveller bold;' (MS, Victoria Library at the University of Toronto, *1845??*). Alongside SC's original MS, Ernest Hartley Coleridge has transcribed and punctuated the poem, and noted: 'Lines in Sara Coleridge's handwriting – appended to a note referring to the pagination of STC's *Literary Remains*'. He speculated 'Do the lines refer to the mingled web of STC's literary fabric? The juxtaposition of precious ore with debris of rock and dregs and rubble?' SC's draft MS is entirely unpunctuated, and can be reconstructed by simply omitting the punctuation; for the copy-text I have in this case used EHC's transcript.

The date of the poem is uncertain, but the likeliest addressee is Aubrey de Vere, in which case it is likely to date from 1843–5, like the other poems written under his influence. SC helped HNC with the editing of the four volumes of STC's *Literary Remains* (1836), and used the second volume for the text of STC's *Notes and Lectures upon Shakespeare*, which she edited and brought out in 1849.

Line 7: 'Of fruit as annually glowing' (variant). Line 10: 'Its boughs beset with fruit and flowers' (variant). Line 16: 'Barren and bearing bitter fruit' (variant).

Page 158. 'To a fair young Lady who declared that she and I were coevals' (RB, 1845, 'For A. de V.', and CV3). De Vere was himself twelve years younger than SC. Below the poem is a variant of the fifth verse:

Perchance thy words – I've read them wrong
And this their meaning, thou'lt avow,
That I, who seem t' have lived so long
Am yet no older, Sweet, than thou.

Page 159. 'To a Fair Friend arguing in support of the theory of the reno-vation in a literal sense of the material system' (RB, 1845, 'For A. de V.',), published in *EC*, p. 235, where the poem is followed by this explanatory letter to Miss Morris, dated 8 September 1845:

I have often spoken of you to Mr. de Vere; and yesterday I told him that the views which he was setting forth in regard to the future world, the glorified body, and the new heavens and earth, were in spirit, and to a great degree in form, extremely similar to those I had heard you express and warmly enlarge upon. *I* am much more *dry*, alas! on these subjects; at least, I am aware that my belief must appear very dry and cold to all but those who entertain it. *We* somehow fancy that we are to have a quintessence of all that is exalted and glowing and beautiful in your new-world creed hereafter, only not in the same way. Mr. de Vere can not bear to part with our human body altogether, nor with this beautiful earth with its glorious canopy. He wants to keep these things, but to have them unimaginably raised and purified and glorified! *I* think that *they* must go, but that all the loveliness and majesty and exquisiteness are to be unimag-inably extracted and enshrined in a new, unimaginable form, in another, and to us now, inconceivable state of existence.

In the version SC sent de Vere, she had evidently included a further, penultimate stanza:

Saviour who, from Heav'n descending,
　Tears like man for man to shed,
Heav'nly pow'rs on earth dispending,
　Knew not where to lay His head.

When we view thee as Thou art
Will that sight change our human heart?

De Vere advised her that 'It strikes me the poem would be more complete without the stanza before the last'.

The version of the poem in *EC*, pp. 235–6, has a different last line (recorded also as a variant in the Red Book), 'Destined, in Heaven's great Day, to vanish from our sight?'

Page 160. 'Dreams I. The Lilies' (RB, 1845, 'For A. de V.'). 'I had written in stanza 5 "The radiant lilies by the rough hill side". Mr de Vere says "Except the redundancy of epithet in this line I can find no fault in this very beautiful poem"' (SC).

Page 160. 'Dreams II. Time's Acquittal' (RB, 1846, 'For A. de V.').

Page 162. 'Dreams III. To a Friend' (RB, 1847, 'For A. de V.'). 'This may seem extravagant, but truly represents the feeling of the dream – wherein *the flow of speech* was what chiefly impressed me and seemed almost a distinct thing – abstracted from the speaker – and yet the speaker was there in person too' (SC). The epigraph from Browne does not show up in electronic searches of his works, and may perhaps be a pastiche of Browne by STC.

Line 6: '"placid in its going"' – Wordsworth, *The White Doe of Rylstone*, Canto 1, line 148. Line 66: '"a dear domestic stream"' – Coleridge, 'Recollections of Love', line 25. The whole stanza in STC reads

You stood before me like a thought,
    A dream remembered in a dream.
    But when those meek eyes first did seem
To tell me, Love within you wrought –
    O Greta, dear domestic stream!'

SC's Diary for 13 August 1850 records another vivid dream about de Vere:

On Sunday morning I had a ghastly dream. The dead body of Aubrey de Vere lay in the coffin beside me. It was a corse, and yet de Vere had sense and mind remaining. I sat beside him, talked and took care of him. Then we went forward, as it were, on a journey to convey the body to his friend or for some indefinite purpose. My clothes were dropping off my back and I became more and more impeded and disordered. We stopped at some large farm house – and I arranged my Clothes, leaving the body in charge of the people of the house. After hastily fastening my clothes, I stepped forward again to resume the charge of the living corse. To my agony I found it had been treated as a corse indeed, as a lifeless worthless husk: had been thrust some where under the grate in some stifling hole. I saw indifference to my feelings and invincible obstinacy written on the face of the woman I addressed. The men would come in half an hour, she said carelessly, to carry on the body. I felt as if it were vain even to entreat to have the coffin and body restored to me directly. I strove to think that it was but a senseless corpse after all. In this agony I awoke – the bonds of sleep seemed to be burst by the struggle, and I felt thankful that it was all a dream, and my friend doubtless philosophizing at Tonbridge Wells with his friends the Taylors.

Page 164. 'Asceticism' (RB, *1845?*, 'For A. de V.'). 'No great force of reasoning here against Asceticism. No – but quite as much as some defenders have of late displayed in its favour. Let argument meet argument – sentiment sentiment – sport and badinage be combated with their own weapons' (SC).

After the second stanza SC has ruled the double line with which she usually marked the end of a poem, and it looks as if the third and fourth stanzas are a continuation at a later moment. The start of the poem (at least) seems to be written around the same time as SC's unpublished twelve-page essay on asceticism in the HRC, titled 'Thoughts on Asceticism by a "Rationalist", in search of true Religion, or rather in search of a true *form* of faith already found'. (SC was a 'Rationalist' by dint of her 'Essay on Rationalism', published in 1843 as Appendix C to the fifth edition of STC's *Aids to Reflection*.) This essay has two epigraphs, of which the second comes from de Vere: 'without asceticism the character does not attain its utmost height, and if this elevation is gained at the expense of its full expansion, still is it not better for society that models should exist of every form of excellence?' SC starts her essay by asking 'Is this true Christian philosophy, or does it belong to that peculiar corruption of Christianity commonly called Romanism, which I would define in general as the principle of assigning an undue place to the outward and sensuous in the sphere of religion?'

Page 165. 'Blanco White' (RB, 1845), published as 'To Joseph Blanco White' in *Confessions of an Inquiring Spirit* (1849), p. 241, and in *EC*, pp. 355–6. Joseph Blanco White (1775-1841), a wealthy Spaniard of Irish descent, joined but later abandoned the Roman Catholic priesthood before in 1810 he left Spain for England, where amid struggles of conscience he became successively an Anglican and a Unitarian. He was a poet, editor and man of letters, and a friend of STC and his brother John Duke Coleridge.

'Written after a warm debate on BW's merits and demerits – faults and advantages, and the excuses and causes thereof – with my dear brother-in-law E.C. [Edward Coleridge] at Eton 1845' (SC). 'I have never "defended" Blanco White. But I do *insist* on looking at his virtues and struggles and powers of mind with the naked eye and not through the glass of an opinion concerning his religious opinions. In thus dealing I put forth no new view of Christian justice and toleration – I do but carry out the commonly received view consistently and without vacillation' (SC). 'Men will not believe that BW died a firm believer in a Moral and Intelligent Creator and

Governor to whom our homage and submission is due, because he rejected Revelation (outward) and was unconvinced of the resurrection of man's soul to conscious existence' (SC).

As her three marginal notes above indicate, SC had a troubled and continuing interest in Blanco White. As early as 1826 she was reading his *Practical and Internal Evidence against Catholics* (1825) and recommending it to Derwent. On 18 August 1845 she wrote to John Taylor Coleridge that she was 'reading the autobiography and letters of Blanco White': 'It is a deeply and dreadfully interesting book', she wrote; 'his life in Spain [...] serves strongly to confirm all my prejudices about these Romish practices'. In February 1846 she wrote about White to F.D.Maurice, expressing her disappointment with the article about him in the *Quarterly Review*, and admiring his truthfulness, and the powers of thought and faith he showed during his last illness (see *EC*, pp. 254–5).

SC revised the poem for its publication in the 1849 edition of *Confessions of an Inquiring Spirit* (p. 241):

To Joseph Blanco White

Could'st thou so calmly, tried one, yield thy breath
Void of the Christian's sure and certain hope?
Didst thou to earth confine our being's scope,
Yet, fixed on One Supreme with fervent faith,
As though intent t'escape eternal scath
Shun the smooth worldly ways that hell-ward slope?
O thou light-searching spirit that didst grope
In such bleak shadows here, 'twixt life and death,
For thee have I borne witness, though in ruth,
Like thee by blame unmoved – dare hope and pray
That thou, released from that ill frame of clay,
Thine earth-born clog, renewed in heavenly youth,
Mayst find that bliss untold, 'mid endless day,
Awaits each earnest soul that lived for Truth.

The poem appears in the 1849 *Confessions of an Inquiring Spirit* as a footnote to a passage in which SC attacks commentators who assume of STC 'that because he had at one time intercourse with B. White, and strove to infuse into him truly philosophical and Catholic views, he should be set forth as a kindred spirit with that "most unhappy man of men", unhappy in the constitution of his mind and in its circumstances, who, however, spite of the blindness that came upon him respecting the divinity of Christ and a personal resurrection, preserved a faith in the One Supreme Being – a sense of fealty and unconditional submission to Him, as the Creator and Moral Governor of the world, I doubt not vastly more sincere and sustaining than that of numbers who think they do God service by transforming his doctrine into

Atheism, and conforming his life and morals to their view of his opinions' (p. xxx). The quoted phrase 'most unhappy man of men' comes from Wordsworth's sonnet 'To Toussaint L'Ouverture', line 1.

Page 165. 'To a Friend who wished to give me half her sleep' (RB, *1845?*, 'For A. de V.'). Line 10 suggests that the friend may be the poet de Vere in female disguise.

Page 166. 'To a Friend who prayed, that my heart might still be young' (RB, 1845, 'For A. de V.').

'Mr de Vere proposes [for the ending]

> Ill omened daring! – Thou – my Friend – and I,
> Bending will hear the shrill shaft o'er us fly:
> Then lift our heads and sigh for those who find
> That Love is ever wakeful and not blind.' (SC).

At first ended thus:

> Philario's eye once once could love inspire
> Time's scarce-perceivèd hand has quenched their fire –
> He still young-hearted seeks with stealthy aim
> To seize Love's quiver and secure his flame
> But scorched himself and wounded sighs to find
> That Love is ever wakeful and not blind' (SC).

Line 14: 'moon-lighted all day long' – de Vere, 'The Search after Proserpine', scene IV, 'Or Primroses moon-lighted all day long'. Line 17: 'have their closes' – George Herbert, 'Virtue', lines 9-12: 'Sweet spring, full of sweet days and roses, / A box where sweets compacted lie; / My music shows ye have your closes, / And all must die'. Line 29: 'Love is ever wakeful and *not* blind' – compare 'Passion is blind not Love', above, p. 186.

Page 167. 'On reading my Father's "Youth and Age"' (RB, *1845?*, 'For A. de V.'). In her co-edited volume of STC's poems, SC's note on 'Youth and Age' suggests that the composition of the poem reflected its theme, in that (she argues) its opening seventeen-line verse paragraph was written far later than the 32 lines of its final two paragraphs. Coleridge's poem is a lament for the lost powers of his youth.

Page 168. 'To a little weanling Babe, who returned a kiss with great eagerness' (RB, *1845?*, 'For A. de V.', and MS, undated).

'A. de Vere adds this stanza.

> Never be the sweet fount dry! –
> Ah! but there are darker dangers
> For the too adventurous rangers
> Near the sunnier Castaly,
> May the indulgent lips that suffer

Thine, no poison take or proffer;
And, if thy peace they draw from thee,
Feed thee with their purity' (SC).

Neither of the two texts of the poem is dated, and its subject suggests that it might date from SC's grief in 1832–3 when because of ill-health she was forced prematurely to stop breastfeeding Edith (see note to 'Darling Sister Edith', pp. 238–9, below); but the heading 'For A. de V.' places it later, according to SC's prefatory note in the Red Book.

The MS version has a number of variants: in the first stanza it reads 'Darling Babe' (line 1), 'Smooth it is and soft as silk' (line 5), and 'these banks' (line 7); in line 12 'Gentle woman's words'; and for lines 13-14 'May no lip, whence love and blindness / Make thee long for streams of kindness'.

Page 168. 'Dream-love' (RB, *1845?*, 'For A. de V.', and CV3), published in Griggs, pp. 220–1. SC has written an alternative version of the first verse in the margin:

Ah yes! I know 'tis all a dream
The union of thy heart and mine –
Round thee the noon-day splendours beam
Whilst I am dark, in life's decline
But yet a moment let it shine
Of fancied love this flickering gleam –
For one brief moment yet be mine –
Nay be not such but only seem.

Line 28: '"The cold phosphoric fires decay"' – from George Crabbe, *Tales of the Hall*, Book VIII, 'The Sisters', lines 855–6: 'Till, as the morning sunbeams glow, / The cold phosphoric fires decay'. SC pasted Crabbe's signature into her first Commonplace Book, and frequently wrote admiringly about him, as for instance in a letter of 17 June 1846: 'The *Tales of the Hall* are what I now like best of all his sets of poems. In my earlier days I did not perceive half their merits, the fine observation of life, the tender sympathy with human sorrow, the gentle smile at human weakness, the humour, the pathos, the firm, almost stern morality, the excellent, clear, pure diction, and the touches of beauty (as I think) interspersed here and there' (*EC*, pp. 256–7, to Mrs Richard Townsend).

Page 169. 'To my Son' (RB, *1845?*).

Page 171. 'Tennyson's "Lotos Eaters" with a new conclusion' (RB, *1840??*). Tennyson himself provided the poem with a new conclusion when he included it in his 1842 *Poems*, substituting a new last strophe for the one from which SC quotes. This might suggest that SC's poem was written before 1842, and it lacks the 'For A. de V.' tag which accompanies most of the poems of 1843–5. On the other hand, SC attended most closely to

Tennyson's works for her 1848 article on *The Princess* in the *Quarterly Review*; and discussed his work frequently with de Vere, whom she thought too extravagant an admirer. Because the date is uncertain, the poem has been left in this edition in the same place it appears in RB, alongside the two poems on Crashaw. The quoted phrases from the 1832 version of 'The Lotos-Eaters' ('T') all come from the seventh and final strophe of the 'Choric Song' (from which SC does not quote the three final lines). Lines 1–8 (and, similarly, 35–7) in SC are taken from lines 126–33 in T (T has 'alarm' not [']alarms' and 'tossing ocean'); lines 12-13 from lines 153-4 in T ('We'll lift no more' [in T]); lines 26-34 from lines 159–67 in T ('foamwhite' in T, and slightly different punctuation); line 38 from line 139 in T.

Page 173. 'Crashaw's Poetry' (RB, *1845?*, 'For A. de V.'). The asterisks and notes are SC's, and to judge from the MS she meant the jocular notes to appear on the page with the poem. All the phrases in quotation marks come from Crashaw's poems, most frequently (on six occasions) from 'On a Prayer Book sent to Mrs M.R'.

Writing to Mrs Townsend in September 1847, SC praised Crashaw as a writer 'whose sacred poetry I think more truly poetical than any other, except Milton and Dante'. Both Wordsworth and Coleridge were admirers, she wrote, 'but then neither Quarles nor Crashaw would be much liked by the modern general reader. They would be thought queer and extravagant' (*EC*, pp. 320–1). In an 1849 letter to de Vere she recommended Vaughan's poems: 'They are very sweet, some lovely, but have less power and thought than Herbert's, less perfect execution than Crashaw's' (*EC*, p. 386).

Page 174. 'On the same' (RB, *1845?*).

Page 175. 'Toil not for burnish'd gold that poorly shines' (RB, *1845?*, 'For A. de V.').

Epigraph from de Vere – on 13 September 1845 de Vere copied into SC's album the final six lines of his sonnet 'Free born, it is my purpose to die free':

Are there no flowers on earth, in heaven no stars,
That we should rest on such low things our trust?
Let me have noble toils if toil I must,
The Patriot's task or Friendship's sacred cares:
But they beside my board shall break no crust
Who sell their birthright for a feast of dust.

Epigraph from Horace – Odes 3.1 ('Odi profanum vulgus et arceo'), lines 47–8. These are the last lines of the Ode and could be translated as 'Why exchange this Sabine vale for more laborious luxury?' The quoted phrases in the second verse (lines 20 and 21) come from Wordsworth's 'To a Young Lady who had been reproached for taking long walks in the country', lines 13-14: 'Thy thoughts and feelings shall not die, / Nor leave thee, when grey hairs are nigh'. Line 23: '"low things"'– probably alluding to Wordsworth's *The Excursion*, Book VII, lines 1046–7: 'Trusting that not incongruously I blend / Low things with lofty'.

SC has three pieces of marginalia to this poem, beside the first and third verses, and at the end. (1) 'Do not let the badness of the poetry blind you to the goodness of the sense, nor the want of authority in the teacher to the truth of the lesson, nor of subtlety and novelty in the argument to its practical usefulness' (SC's marginal note beside the first verse). (2) Beside the third verse SC has written three lines from Burns's 'Epistle to James Smith': 'The wand of pow'r then seek to wield / For once that five and forty's spield / See crazy, weary, joyless Eild etc'. Burns's stanza reads in full:

> The magic wand then let us wield;
> For once that five-an'-forty's speeld,
> See crazy, weary, joyless, Eild
>   Wi' wrinkled face,
> Comes hostin, hirplin owre the field,
>   Wi' creeping pace.

(3) 'Quare vis procrastinare propositum tuum? Surge, et in instante incipe, et dic: nunc tempus est faciendi, nunc tempus est pugnandi – Age, age nunc frater, quicquid agere potes: nunc tempus est valde pretiosum. Thos a Kempis' (SC has written this passage under the lines she drew to mark the end of a poem). The quotation could be translated 'Why do you want to procrastinate on this issue? Rise up, and start right now, and say: now is the time for action, now is the time to fight – Act, act now brother, do whatever you can: now is the precious time for exertion'. It joins together three passages from *The Imitation of Christ*; first, from verse 5 of chapter 22 (up to 'tempus est pugnandi'); secondly, from verse 8 of chapter 23 (up to 'quicquid agere potes'); and finally from verse 5 of chapter 23. SC has altered À Kempis's 'nunc charissime' ('now dearest one') to 'nunc frater' (now brother), so it is possible that the poem and the marginal note glance at the irregularities of her two brothers, Derwent when young, and Hartley throughout his life; but the second verse suggests a younger addressee than Derwent or Hartley (who in any case went grey prematurely). Most likely this poem, like 'To my Son', is an advice poem addressed to Herbert Coleridge. De Vere sent SC a copy of À Kempis's *Valley of Lilies* in October 1851 (*EC*, p. 527).

Page 176. 'Sketch from Life. Morning Scene. Sept 22 1845' (RB, 'For A. de V.'). Line 1: 'a windladen billow' – from de Vere's 'Dolores. (Scene in a Madhouse)', where the phrase is part of the refrain: 'Whence caught you, sweet Mourner, the swell of that song? / "From the arch of yon windladen billow"' (lines 10-11, 23–4, 36–7, 49–50).

Page 177. 'A Boy's complaint of Dr Blimber' (RB, *1845?*). Dr Blimber runs a school in Dickens's *Dombey and Son*.

Pages 177-81. These five poems inspired by or derived from *Phantasmion* come together in sequence in the Red Book. None of them appeared in the 1837 first edition of the book, and only 'L'Envoy' in the new 1874 edition, having already first been printed in *EC* in 1873 (1874 edition, p. 136). They are followed by a paragraph headed 'Moral of *Phantasmion*' (see below).

Page 177. 'L'Envoy to "Phantasmion"' (RB, 1845, 'For A. de V.'), published in *EC*, p. 136, and *Phantasmion* (second edition, 1874), p. ix. Edith Coleridge notes that the poem was 'written in a copy of *Phantasmion* about the year 1845' – very likely de Vere's copy in view of its being 'For A. de V.'. The published versions add a long dash at the end of line 4, and remove the emphasis on '*him*' in line 8.

Page 178. 'Feydeleen to Zelneth' (RB, *1845?*). 'For *Phantasmion*' (SC). The fairy Feydeleen, the 'Spirit of the Flowers', consoles Zelneth about her unrequited love for Phantasmion. The reflections on age might be thought to reflect less on Zelneth, who is a young woman, than on SC herself at the likely time of writing. SC used the phrase 'the sere and yellow leaf' (alluding to *Macbeth*, V.iii.25) to refer to her own state in the opening lines of 'On reading my Father's "Youth and Age"', above, p. 167: 'I behold the sere and yellow leaf / I'm fallen into' (lines 2-3).

Page 179. 'Song of Leucoia' (RB, *1845?*). 'For *Phantasmion*' (SC). Leucoia is a very young woman throughout *Phantasmion*, and she ends happily married to Ulander: so it is hard to see how the song applies to her character. Line 4: '"whose hue, angry and brave"' – George Herbert, 'Virtue', lines 5-8: 'Sweet rose, whose hue angry and brave / Bids the rash gazer wipe his eye; / Thy root is ever in its grave, / And thou must die'.

Page 180. 'Song for "Phantasmion"' (RB, *1845?*). SC gives no indication of the singer or the place in the story. She seems later to have considered including this poem in 'Howithorn', noting 'Ere I knew thee' (presumably for 'Ere I loved thee') between sets of draft verses (see pp. 206–7, above).

Page 180. 'Zelneth. Love unreturned' (RB, *1845?*). 'For *Phantasmion*' (SC). In the book, Zelneth is in love with Phantasmion, who looks on her kindly but not amorously. Between this poem and the next in the Red Book comes the paragraph headed 'Moral of *Phantasmion*':

Any Tale that represents human life, even in fairy-land, its joys and sorrows, troubles and trials, successes and failures, will have its moral, and the more truthful, if its aim is not [to] embody a particular moral, but to show things as they are, and let the moral follow of its own accord. This Tale was not written as an allegory to convey some one truth, moral, political, or philosophical; yet many morals are illustrated by the several parts of the story; – nay the whole is shaped by the moral instincts of one educated in a Christian land. Glandreth, Dorimant and Magnart are victims of inordinate ambition – Albinian and Anthemmina of ill-regulated passion – Zalia and Arzene, as so often happens in real life, of the ill-doings of others, together with a certain weakness – a want of sagacity – of resisting energy in themselves. Karadan, in his character and history, exemplifies the two last morals. Zalia ought to have refused the hand of Dorimant: Arzene ought not to have exposed her own life for the sake of one self-devoted boy, who had left her to pursue a hopeless passion, she having other children. Zelneth partakes of Anthemmina's fault and of its punishment; but her fault is less and so is her punishment. Leucoia suffers, but less keenly, – more negatively, as her folly is of a more passive and negative character. Phantasmion obtains the success which bright gifts of nature, united with energy, courage and perseverance almost ensure. Iarine is an example of the Scriptural saying, *Blessed are the meek, for they shall inherit the Earth!*

Page 181. 'Matthew VI.28-9' (RB, *1845?*). Like the 'Scriptural saying' exemplified by Iarine at the end of the 'Moral of Phantasmion' (Matthew 5:5), these verses come from the Sermon on the Mount: 'And why take ye thought for raiment? Consider the lilies of the field, how they grow; they toil not, neither do they spin: / And yet I say unto you, That even Solomon in all his glory was not arrayed like one of these'. Compare SC's Diary entry for 30 August 1850, talking of 'a little flashy dashy article' which her son had written: 'There is a swing in these youthful productions – a joyous flippancy which Solomon in all his wisdom and knowledge could not have rivalled – any more than the cleverest human architect could build a bird's nest.'

Page 183. 'Prayer for Tranquillity' (RB, *1845?*, and CV3), published in *Dora Wordsworth: Her Book*, ed. F.V.Morley (1924), p. 168. This poem is the last entry in Dora Wordsworth's album, where it is signed and dated 'Sara Coleridge, September 17 1850'; but its place in RB and at the end of CV3 suggest that it was written earlier. Possibly it was sent to Dora as her health declined, and after her death in 1847 her husband Edward Quillinan felt it would be appropriate to enter it in the album.

Line 5: I have substituted CV3's 'tumultuous' for RB's 'tempestuous' to avoid the repetition; RB has 'fires of passion' as an alternative to 'tempest passions' in line 6, but 'send away' agrees better with tempests than fires. For line 8 RB and Dora's album agree on 'Where all our earthly troubles cease' (but 'When' for 'Where' in Dora's album), while CV3 has 'Which nought can raise and nought decrease'. RB has a version of this line – '(Which nought can mar and nought decrease)' – below line 8, but the parentheses and grammatical sense suggest that it is an alternative to line 8 and not a new line 9. For an unpacking of the idea in the parenthetical line, see 'O change that strain with man's best hopes at strife', above, pp. 187–8.

Page 183. 'The melancholy Prince' (RB, *1845?*, and CV3). 'Written for *Phantasmion*' (SC) – but also, like 'Ere I loved thee', considered for inclusion in 'Howithorn' (see note to 'Song for "Phantasmion"', above, p. 235). Line 16: 'unlovely' (RB) – 'so hateful' (CV3).

Page 184. 'Zelneth's Song in Magnart's Garden' (RB, *1845?*). 'For *Phantasmion*' (SC). The song was probably intended to conclude chapter 11, after Zelneth discovers that the disguised Phantasmion is in love not with her but Iarine. '"O Leucoia!" she cried, "thy channel once was full, though now the stream is dried at the fountain: but mine has ever been despised, unvisited; the current winds another way, and will not flow there"' (*Phantasmion*, p. 95).

Page 185. 'Children' (RB, *1845?*). 'For *Phantasmion*' (SC). SC has asterisked line 24 and noted '*Phantasmion* p. 149', the page on which the song 'How gladsome is a child' appears in the 1837 edition. The sixth verse of this poem is the final one of the song in 1837 (see p. 125, above).

Lines 25–6: 'I dread the ghastly witch and the goblin of the dark' – SC records her own childish fears in her unfinished autobiography: 'During my Grasmere visit [aged five] I used to feel frightened at night, on account of the darkness. I then was a stranger to the whole host of night-agitators – ghosts, goblins, demons, devils, boggles, burglarists, elves and witches. Horrid ghastly tales & ballads, of which crowds afterwards came in my way, had not yet cast their shadows over my mind. And yet I was terrified of the dark...' (Mudge, pp. 265–6).

Page 186. 'Passion is blind not Love: *her* wondrous might' (published in *Biographia Literaria* (1847), i. clxxxiv). This poem concludes SC's 184-page introduction to the edition, and implicitly rebuts the anticipated objection that filial love has made it impossible for her to write accurately about her own father (see also pp. clxxxii–clxxxiv).

Line 9: '"dread abode"' – 'Or draw his frailties from their dread abode', Thomas Gray, 'Elegy Written in a Country Churchyard', line 126. For SC's views on Gray, see L.N. Broughton, *Sara Coleridge and Henry Reed* (1937), pp. 63-73.

Page 187. 'O change that strain with man's best hopes at strife,', published in *Aids to Reflection* (sixth edition, 2 vols, 1848), ii. 280–1. SC added 'Extracts from a New Treatise on Regeneration' to this new 1848 edition (ii. 249-322): these 73 pages are all that has yet been published of her projected theological magnum opus. The poem is part of a discussion of 'The Indefectibility of the Regenerate Estate'. SC takes issue with the implication of Keble's lines from *The Christian Year* which stand as epigraph to her poem: 'They who say that a man may fall from the regenerate estate, the highest state of grace attainable in this life, inferentially though unintentionally represent God as an author of Absolute Decrees, an arbitrary awarder of destruction or salvation: when, according to their theory, He allows some of the justified time to forfeit their inheritance, and rescues others by a timely deliverance from spiritual chance and change' (pp. 279-80). The lines from Keble and her own verses follow this sentence.

'This address is to a phantom Harmonist, with whom I can speak as freely as my Uncle, Mr. Southey, does with the phantom Sir Thomas More, of his *Colloquies*' (SC) – see Southey's *Sir Thomas More; or, colloquies on the Progress and Prospects of Society* (2 vols, 1829). The 'gentle Harmonist' in line 29 seems to be Keble.

Epigraph: the final stanza of 'Eight Sunday After Trinity' ('Prophet of God, arise and take') from Keble's *The Christian Year* (lines 49-52). SC thought poems on religious subjects 'the easiest of all to write commonplaceishly – the hardest to write worthily in', and did not greatly admire Keble's poetry: 'Mr Keble and his friends *adorn* doctrine with fine feathers of poetical diction and imagery', and Keble in his verses uses incidents as 'just so many pegs and hooks' on which he 'can hang his web of religious sentiment' (*EC*, p. 260).

Line 2: 'A recreant strain that wrongs the steadfast soul!' – 'A recreant harp, that sings of fear / And heaviness in Clifford's ear' (SC). SC's note cites Wordsworth's 'Song at the Feast of Brougham Castle', lines 102–3.

Line 40: 'Has He not promised His beloved rest?' – 'Rev.iii.20. This text shows that the free will admits grace into the soul; that it is not *in* the soul, before the will has consented to its entrance' (SC). The verse reads 'Behold, I stand at the door, and knock: if any man hear my voice, and open the door, I will come in to him, and will sup with him, and he with me'.

Page 188. 'O vain expenditure! unhallowed waste!', published in *Aids to Reflection* (sixth edition, 2 vols, 1848), ii. 313–14. SC is arguing that given the limited capacities of the infant, regeneration cannot be accomplished by infant baptism. Compare 'Mystic Doctrine of Baptism' above, pp. 193–4. Line 24: '"Sure as day to night"' – perhaps alluding to Polonius's 'it must follow as the night the day / Thou canst not then be false to any man' (Hamlet, 1.iii.78–9).

Page 189. 'Darling Edith' (CV3, 1848, and RB, 1851). The copy text is from CV3, written in SC's hand, and dated 'Feby 1848', at which point Edith was 15; the version in RB is the final poem in the book, and is in Edith Coleridge's hand. She has noted, it seems mistakenly, 'Written by Sara Coleridge in 1851'. SC first used something like the rhyme and metric of this poem in a little verse 'To Baby Edith' in CV2. It began

Good morn to darling Edith
Whom nurse so fondly feedeth:
    May all she eats
    Be filled with sweets,
And sweet the life she leadeth!

An earlier, deleted, first line read 'Farewell my dear little Edith', most likely when Sara was too ill to breastfeed her.

Page 190. 'First chorus in "The Agamemnon" of Æschylus' (RB, 1848). This is the only poem in a section headed 'Translations from the Classics', to which SC prefaces the following statement:

> I think it was in February 1848, or early that year, that my brother-in-law J.T.C put me upon writing an article for the Quarterly. John's proposal was well meant and kind, and I gained a little sum by the article which led to my producing another on Dyce's Beaumont and Fletcher. I was at that time intent upon translating the Agamemnon of Æschylus into verse. I have since thought my time would have been better employed in the mere attempt at an Æschylean translation, than in criticising Tennyson's 'Princess', respecting which my opinion was of that intermediate cast, which disgusts *parties* on both sides. Some of my friends thought the piece scarce deserving a detailed examination: while the Poet's young enthusiastic admirers would endure no censure of it, and thought all criticism poor and inadequate, which did not represent the Poem as a sublime and pregnant allegory. How an allegory so obscure as this must be if it be an allegory at all, the sense of which never presented itself to readers in general, and was reserved for the discovery of a favoured few, is in my judgment, no successful product of the Muse of Poetry, and I cannot think The Princess will ever hold a higher rank amongst the works of genius than I assigned it in consequence of the explanation that Lilia means the Spirit of the Age, and Ida – I protest I know not what she was said to personify. Perhaps *she* was the Spirit of the Age and Lilia that of the Age gone by. But I talk in the dark and it matters not. What I meant to record only was that, as the critique of the Princess appeared in the Quarterly of March 1848, I broke off my Agamemnon attempt just before, and never afterwards had leisure to resume it. Over leaf I shall give the fragment of the Translation.

SC had for some time been interested in the problems of presenting Greek drama in the nineteenth century. In some diary pages from 1835 she criticised Thomas Talfourd's *Ion*, a success of the day: 'the spirit of the piece is exclusively modern. People did not "sleep and brood o'er their own hearts" in the days of Sophocles and Æschylus. But what could an imitation of a Greek Play by a modern Englishman be good for [...] A story really like the Oedipus Tyrannus or Antigone written at this time of day would be like an Automaton Venus made in leather; and moved by springs'.

At the end of the RB translation SC writes 'caetera desunt – eheu!' ('the rest is wanting – alas!'). On the following pages are transcribed 70 lines of variant readings, headed 'Variations'.

Pages 192-4. 'Poems written for a book of Dialogues on the Doctrines of grace' (RB, *1850-1*). SC refers to a work titled 'Regeneration', on which she worked intensely in the last few years of her life, but only the 'Extracts from a New Treatise on Regeneration' in the 1848 sixth edition of *Aids to Reflection* (ii. 249-322) were ever published. She wrote in her diary for 19 May 1850 that 'I have been going on with the Reg[eneration] book but I fear I shall be obliged to give in – cannot accomplish it in time without my nerves giving way. This will be disappointment to me, as P[ickering] seemed willing to undertake it – almost pleased, I *fancied*, with it'. Nevertheless, she continued to work on it, and left about 500 pages of manuscript in various stages of completion, much of it almost ready for a publisher. Some of her drafts are dated as late as November 1851.

I. 'While disputants for victory fight' (RB and MS). These verses are the conclusion of dialogue V of 'On the Incarnation of our Lord Jesus Christ in relation to Time', the fifth of the seven dialogues which form *Regeneration*, part 1, chapter 1. In the manuscript the lines are attributed to 'Irenia', and line 2 reads 'think to fill the world with light' instead of 'hope to fill'. For another reflection on the conduct of theological controversy, see SC's 'Preliminary Observations' to the 'Extracts from … Regeneration' in *Aids to Reflection* (ii. 249–58).

II. 'Water can but rise to its own level' (RB and MS). These lines come at the end of dialogue V of the 'Introduction to the Dialogues on Regeneration', and are spoken by Markwright: 'Exeunt severally. Markwright murmuring to himself as follows'. The MS has 'subtle bonds' instead of 'subtle bands'.

III. 'Reason' (RB and MS). These verses come from a section of *Regeneration* comparing 'esoteric and exoteric doctrine'. They stand at the head of a chapter titled 'Exoteric', and are followed by a note from SC: 'The reader will goodnaturedly pardon this confident boast and bold assumption, that we have Reason on our side, looking on it as poetical licence. We *hope* however that in the end he will regard [it] as a prolepsis verified in the course of the argument'.

IV. 'Mystic Doctrine of Baptism' (RB only). Much of SC's theological speculation and controversial writing in the second half of the 1840s had centred on baptism, in particular her opposition to what she saw as the Roman Catholic 'mystic doctrine of baptism' (see, among many instances in the life and letters, *EC*, pp. 250–2, 416–19, and 429–34). On 1 November 1849 she wrote to DC that 'the more I think and read, the deeper is my conviction that my father was right. He disclaims the belief that the spirit could be imparted "to an unconscious subject by human ministry"'. STC's discussion of baptism in the 1843 *Aids to Reflection* occupies Volume 1, pp. 281-303. SC set out her own arguments at length in the 'Essay on Rationalism' in Volume 2 of the 1843 *Aids to Reflection* (pp. 335-556); this 'Essay' was reprinted with some expansions in the

1848 edition of the *Aids*, together with 'Extracts from a New Treatise on Regeneration'. She also touched on the subject in the introduction to *Biographia Literaria* (1847): 'My father, as I understand him, continued to deny that the gift of baptism is a spiritual re-creation preceding actual faith or any moral capability, – an introduction of the spirit into the soul, which it passively undergoes, as the dead cage receives the living bird, or a lodgement of the Spirit within it irrespectively of its own moral state […] He looked upon it as an external grant, called regeneration in virtue of that which it is its object to promote and secure, a grant which comes into effect gradually, as the will yields to the pressure of the Spirit from without, but which may be made of none effect by the will's resistance' (i. lxxxi-lxxxii).

V. 'Baptism' (RB only). The emphasis in the poem is on the new life, yet to be lived, into which the Christian has been baptised.

Page 195. '[From "Regeneration"]' (MS, *1850-1*). These lines form the end of one of the dialogues. The second stanza is fragmentary only, and the lacunae in lines 5 and 8 appear thus in the MS. Before the verses one of the speakers, Una, has been discussing 'Christian stability': 'Still it is not the root – this doctrine of Christian stability is not the root of the true Gospel doctrine of regeneration: it is rather the topmost branch that looks up to the sky. We cannot behold it without looking up into the clear blue of heaven. It is one with the peace that passes understanding'.

Page 195. 'Missionary Poem' (MS, *1850-1*). This uncompleted poem about spiritual regeneration was written on cancelled sheets of the 'Regeneration Dialogues', and almost certainly intended eventually to be a part of them. The poem is not complete, and there are various drafts of the first stanza in particular. The lines given here as the incomplete third stanza appear on a separate sheet, and it is only my conjecture that they were a rough draft for the continuation of the poem.

One version of the first stanza has a different landscape:

Lost in dark labyrinths under ground
A weary wight sinks down in prayer
No light he sees – he hears no sound
Save echoes of his own despair
But oh what joy a sudden beaming
Pierces the cave's sepulchral gloom
Forward he springs – to where this light is streaming
Soon to be rescued from the tomb.

Elsewhere in the MS papers for 'Regeneration' SC has carefully transcribed four lines of Pope probably related to the setting of this poem: 'The swain in barren deserts with surprise / Sees lilies spring and sudden verdure rise; / And starts amid the thirsty wilds to hear / New falls of water murm'ring in his ear' ('Messiah, A Sacred Eclogue, in Imitation of Virgil's Pollio', lines 67-70). SC's first published work, in 1822, had been her anonymous translation of the *Account of the Abipones, an Equestrian People of Paraguay*, by the Jesuit missionary Martin Dobrizhoffer.

Page 196. '[From Sara Coleridge's Journal, September 1850]' (MS, 1850). From the journals which SC kept between 1848 and 1852. Elsewhere in her journal she notes that 'Edith danced as much as I could wish and even had to refuse' (cited in Griggs, p. 227), so the objection is not to all dancing at all times.

Page 196. '[From a letter to Mrs Derwent Coleridge, 16 January 1852]' (MS, 1852). SC had received from Edward Moxon and C.B. Stutfield various books she needed for the edition of STC's poems she was preparing with Derwent.

Page 197. 'From a letter to Derwent Coleridge, 22 January 1852' (MS, 1852). Derwent had without consulting SC come and taken Poole's picture of STC for the frontispiece of the edition of his poems.

Page 198. 'Doggrel Charm' (MS, 1852). The MS is in Edith Coleridge's hand. Sara Coleridge died on 3 May 1852. Line 2: 'pretermit' – desist from, leave undone.

Appendix: 'Howithorn' (MS, 1848)

I include here my attempts to transcribe the main parts of SC's scheme for the poem. Many of the readings are conjectural or dubious. Notes, marked by asterisks, are my own.

(a) Sept 20 1848
Altamire after the fall* of his wife. Thunder and lightning – the falls come con po morte cadde.

Seized with remorse. Wishes to go to consult his sage Aunt (Queen) Themilda in Temuristan. – Wanders down to lake side. Sees an old man weeping. He had come in a boat to gather a certain herb said to be good to make sleep fruitful – too weary to return. Altamire takes him into a hut. Exchanges his fine cap for the old herdsman's cap – Offers to exchange hair – the old man will not exchange December snows for June fruit and flower blossoms blooms. Hostess glues white locks to cap. Whitens his face. He looks old yet vigorous.

Rows across Lake – arrives moonlight. Descent [?? under] near. Howithorn looking bright and meek – tears on cheek at Charelio's absorption with his love. Altamire thinks her the spirit of his wife. She

---

* She had fallen into the lake.

looks like the moon deity. As if she had left her empty nest. Slid down through the luminous cloud left her bright mantle behind left her [?future] bright with light. Swanlike throat and neck.

Reflection. Marriage tie dissolved not to be reunited suddenly.

Altamire as old man gains entrance to castle. Hears of Invasion of Clorian (father of Charelio). Suddenly throws off his feebleness and flies to arms to assist his father when he finds Charelio make head.

Sept 24

All the subterranean way recesses light with cressets – statues fruit wine conserves Likanare eagerly paces along will not stop till exhausted. Refuses help at the last. Expects many miles again – not a brooklet off the outlet – mouth of the passage [?reached] at with glowing cheek. Livid bright moonlight lighting up the very fruit and flourishing trees.

Description of gorgeous bank of trees – flowering shrubs of a thousand hues. Blue gashed like laburnum – apples and [?quinces] – [?many] clusters of bells –

Troops of peacocks with their trains in various directions – a thousand altogether – swans – Likanare in armour – Charelio in woman's attire meet and do not speak. She is yet uncertain whether he loves her or not.

Howithorn is seen and taken for a spectre by Altamire as he nears in the boat. Afterwards he obtains an interview of the sage Theaura.★

He begs he may be in a dim light on account of the affliction of his eyes.★★ She tells him of Howithorn's sorrow and how she began to reflect that she had not loved Altamire when she met but had neglected him for Charelio. But her senses had left her and she knew nothing after she fell into the lake nor just before.

When it is asked if Charelio returns the love of Likanare this first reveals to Theaura why Charelio wished her sent for – knows not that she has brought in a rival – that the youth in armour is Likanare – shows her too clearly the state of her own heart. By the dim firelight her face glows then sinks as the flame flares up then dies away. Clorian's invasion betrays Likanare to her. Thus the unhappy girl is again in durance and sorrow. Theaura's however is a [?mute] captivity.

Reflection. Likanare's breaking from her faith and pledge brings on her captivity and bondage with Malibar. Such ill must be atoned for.

The concluding scene, Theaura's illness and resignation of Likanare

★ Theaura's name also appears as Themilda and Almantha. Elsewhere SC notes of Theaura, 'Once bright liquid eyes and glowing cheeks. Now pale as [?ash] and hair grey in splendour as Alpine heights amid the blue hot skies and green warm foliage and foliage warm of yellow green seen reflecting to the heavens above.'
★★ Otherwise she would recognise him as her nephew.

to Charelio. She sees heavenly visions – contrast of her dying face with Likanare.

(b)

Interview of Altamire with Howithorn in Lotolia. She speeds out of the Castle [?side]. The very air of Lotolia softens Altamire and cheers him – He takes her for a spectre – She awaits overheard by him the devotion of Charelio for Likanare. Still he thinks Charelio not her brother. But he begins to admire Howithorn in dress he saw her first.

Afterwards he sees her fighting by her brother's side fervent heroine he sees the likeness – he loves her.

She gives him the supposed philtre – It prostrates him in the moment of victory – She is brought into [————] – He revives [? receives] her. She nurses him – They love each other.

(c)

After the marriage that shows Charelio how he departed in armour – Howithorn knew it.

Likanare is held in discussion by the witch – obliged still to feign madness. To put off her armour and appear before her as mad [...] .

Instead of this she rushes down with a [————] way below the rocks and thus escapes [...]. She is passing under in armour (she had arranged her armour to the [??windy way]) while Charelio disguised as a woman is passing above in the skiff – with Howithorn insensible in the boat. She emerges in armour just as they [??reach] to land. They then meet in the palace of Regentine. Aunt of Altamire a fair widow in love with Charelio. A sort of Sappho. Described thus: all her genius kept her not from love's thrall. [...] Howithorn knows them. They know not each other. Regentine knows Charelio through her disguise. Howithorn and Regentine are friends.

(d)

Scheme

Clorian makes war on Cedreth. Sire of Altamire when wife is Zenia.

Part. Charelio sets off after Likanare – but to evade pursuit goes to the home of a lofty dame his [————] and dresses himself as a woman. Then goes by instead to a land opposite the Black Vale. There he hears of the sage queen Almantha – Aunt of Altamire left reigning Queen of [————]. He goes on to her – She knows him and falls in love with him, but unwittingly assists Likanare to come. Likanare has gone forth with Maliber.* Is kept in durance by her – When Charelio comes over

* The witch who captured Likanare.

COLLECTED POEMS

the lake to the Black Vale – presents herself at the garden. She obliges Likanare still to feign madness. She affects to throw herself into the sea. So to escape Charelio when she does not meet at the Black vale where Maliber is [?? Queen]. But she enters thus herself into a hollow in the rocks and passes underneath guarded by an emissary from [————————]. Light floods all the way. Gnomes – [————] Diamonds cressets. Glauria? Celestis. Howithorn passes over in armour. Almantha sends the emissary at Charelio's [?request] to seek a mad lady thinking to cure her and generally restore her to Altamire if on her return she loves him, however deeply he is attached. […]

Index of First Lines

Index of Titles

Fyfield*Books*

Two millennia of essential classics

The extensive Fyfield*Books* list includes

Djuna Barnes *The Book of Repulsive Women and other poems*
edited by Rebecca Loncraine

Elizabeth Barrett Browning *Selected Poems* edited by Malcolm Hicks

Charles Baudelaire *Complete Poems in French and English*
translated by Walter Martin

The Brontë Sisters *Selected Poems*
edited by Stevie Davies

Lewis Carroll *Selected Poems*
edited by Keith Silver

Thomas Chatterton *Selected Poems*
edited by Grevel Lindop

John Clare *By Himself*
edited by Eric Robinson and David Powell

Samuel Taylor Coleridge *Selected Poetry* edited by William Empson and David Pirie

John Donne *Selected Letters*
edited by P.M. Oliver

Oliver Goldsmith *Selected Writings*
edited by John Lucas

Victor Hugo *Selected Poetry in French and English*
translated by Steven Monte

Wyndham Lewis *Collected Poems and Plays* edited by Alan Munton

Charles Lamb *Selected Writings*
edited by J.E. Morpurgo

Ben Jonson *Epigrams and The Forest*
edited by Richard Dutton

Giacomo Leopardi *The Canti with a selection of his prose*
translated by J.G. Nichols

Andrew Marvell *Selected Poems*
edited by Bill Hutchings

Charlotte Mew *Collected Poems and Selected Prose*
edited by Val Warner

Michelangelo *Sonnets*
translated by Elizabeth Jennings, introduction by Michael Ayrton

William Morris *Selected Poems*
edited by Peter Faulkner

Ovid *Amores*
translated by Tom Bishop

Edgar Allan Poe *Poems and Essays on Poetry*
edited by C.H. Sisson

Restoration Bawdy
edited by John Adlard

Rainer Maria Rilke *Sonnets to Orpheus and Letters to a Young Poet*
translated by Stephen Cohn

Christina Rossetti *Selected Poems*
edited by C.H. Sisson

Sir Walter Scott *Selected Poems*
edited by James Reed

Sir Philip Sidney *Selected Writings*
edited by Richard Dutton

Henry Howard, Earl of Surrey *Selected Poems*
edited by Dennis Keene

Algernon Charles Swinburne *Selected Poems*
edited by L.M. Findlay

Oscar Wilde *Selected Poems*
edited by Malcolm Hicks

Sir Thomas Wyatt *Selected Poems*
edited by Hardiman Scott

For more information, including a full list of Fyfield*Books* and a contents list for each title, and details of how to order the books, visit the Carcanet website at www.carcanet.co.uk or email info@carcanet.co.uk